The Great Depression

A Captivating Guide to the Worldwide Economic Depression that Began in the United States, Including the Wall Street Crash, FDR's New deal, Hitler's Rise and More

Free Bonus from Captivating History (Available for a Limited time)

Hi History Lovers!

Now you have a chance to join our exclusive history list so you can get your first history ebook for free as well as discounts and a potential to get more history books for free! Simply visit the link below to join.

Captivatinghistory.com/ebook

Also, make sure to follow us on:

Twitter: @Captivhistory

Facebook: Captivating History:@captivatinghistory

Contents

Introduction

The stock market crash of 1929 didn't cause the Great Depression by itself, but it is a powerful symbolic starting point to the greatest economic disaster of the twentieth century. On that dark day in October 1929, fortunes were lost and fear of financial insecurity rose throughout the United States and the world. In 1932, the low point of the Depression, as much as a third of Americans were out of work and even more people were unemployed in other countries. The stock market reached its lowest point ever and wouldn't rise to its pre-Depression levels for almost twenty years.

The scale of the crisis demanded new ways of coping and new ideas about the role of government. The ideas that had dominated American thought about the relationship between the economy and government were now viewed to be outdated at best, dangerous at worst. Notions such as laissez faire and self-made men were eclipsed by ideas of government regulation and community involvement. More than any other person in the United States, Franklin D. Roosevelt and his New Deal changed the United States government in fundamental ways.

That sense of community helped many Americans deal with the harsh realities of the Depression. Citizens joined numerous groups and political parties in an effort to feel useful again. The government also encouraged such organization and many professions received government money to foster such community building.

Citizens not only joined groups looking for a purpose and a connection to their fellow people, but also looked toward cultural traditions and institutions to help identify what it meant to be an American, especially in a time of such uncertainty. Though an extraordinary time of hardship, the era of the Great Depression highlighted a vibrant culture. Jobs and money may have been difficult to come by, but people still watched movies and listened to radio programs. They read books and went to dance halls. In short, people still found ways to entertain themselves even in the most difficult of circumstances.

The culture of the Depression took on multiple characteristics. In some cases, it was a critique of American society, especially of capitalism and the consumer culture of the previous decade. In other cases, there was a drive to discover the real America, an idealized rural, traditional America when life was simpler and less concerned with manufactured material goods. A final aspect of the cultural landscape of the Depression was a drive to escape from the troubles of the present day. Wild fantasies and amazing flights of imagination were some of the most popular pieces produced during the era.

The financial collapse of the United States spread around the globe and deepened crises all over the world, particularly in Western Europe. The continent was still recovering from the First World War when the Great Depression unfolded. Germany was especially hit hard by the economic freefall. That nation's ability to pay off its war debt, difficult in the best of times, was non-existent during the Depression. The new Weimar government was dedicated to democracy, but as circumstances continued to deteriorate, new, darker movements spread throughout Germany. Eventually, Germany was consumed by an evil that plunged the world into its largest war ever.

It was the battle to curb the fascist threat that finally ended the Great Depression. Economic recovery had been slow through much of the 1930s, but as Europe prepared for World War II, American industry met the demand for their allies. When the United States was drawn into the war by the attack on Pearl Harbor, the Great Depression was but a memory.

That memory, however, impacted an entire generation of Americans. After World War II, people still dealt with a scarcity mentality. Public policy was also driven by the fear of another depression starting once all of the wartime boosts to the economy slowed down. Keeping Americans working was the number one domestic policy after the war. When the soldiers came home from Europe, the hope was they would find a job.

If that didn't happen, the government made it possible for thousands of GIs to attend college and defer unemployment. Unfortunately, as the time between the present and the Depression becomes more and more distant, some of the lessons of the era are all but forgotten. While policies and agencies are still in place to prevent another full-blown depression, some of the same practices, or very similar practices, are occurring. Risky business behaviors, challenges to democracy, and shifts in the manufacturing economy all point to a very uncertain future.

Chapter 1: Causes of the Great Depression 1918-1929

The Great Depression didn't occur overnight but was rather a decade in the making. A case can be made for an even longer time frame, focusing on the boom and bust nature of the American economy through the nineteenth and twentieth centuries. That is a discussion better left to economic history. Instead of such a macro examination of the origins of the Great Depression, for brevity's sake, this work focuses on events from the end of the First World War until late in 1929 to shed light on what led to the great global economic crisis of the twentieth century.

The Treaty of Versailles, which ended World War I, had many unintended consequences including the effect on the global economy. One of the key provisions of the treaty was that Germany was not only held entirely responsible for the war, but Germany was the principal nation to make reparations to the allied nations. Germany was already reeling from the military defeat and collapse of their government, but their economy was destroyed from the war. Within Germany, starvation was a real concern. Making a dire situation even worse was that another key provision of the treaty was the confiscation of key German territory. Not only was the nation reduced by a third, but much of the land taken away was the heart of German manufacturing. Asking Germany to repay such a vast sum of money was an impossible condition that was never going to be met.

That didn't stop the allies, especially France and Great Britain, from demanding payment. Part of the reason the French and British were relentless on getting their money from Germany was because of the United States demanding repayment of loans that they had given to the allied powers. The Germans were crippled by the amount of money they needed to pay the allies, and while France and Britain weren't in such dire straits, the debt they carried after the war was a drag on their economies as well.

The solution relied on the United States and their willingness to forgive the war debt. Unfortunately for all European nations, the United States wouldn't budge. The president of the United States, Calvin Coolidge, when asked about forgiving the European debt replied, "They borrowed the money, didn't they? They need to repay it." The long-term effect of this stance was to retard global economic growth. Though much of the United States economy was healthy throughout the 1920s, the limits on foreign markets because of their respective national debt eventually hurt the United States economy.

The first segment of the economy to feel the effects of the global slowdown was farming. The end of the war saw the demand for US farm products plunge, due to European nations focused on reviving their own agriculture and becoming less reliant on foreign aid. The reduction in demand was so severe that farmers were incurring heavy losses throughout much of the 1920s. The US Senate attempted to help farmers by fixing prices on certain agricultural goods, providing funds for farmers to *not* cultivate in certain cases, and for the government to buy surplus goods to sell on the international market. On two occasions, Calvin Coolidge vetoed the measure, arguing that such measures were anti-American.

The rest of the American economy was relatively strong through the 1920s, but key industries were showing signs of slowing down by mid-decade. The coal and steel industries, two of the biggest parts of the economy, were reducing production in large part because the nation's railways were not expanding at the same rate as they had been. In addition, the nation's railways were experiencing a decline in ridership due to the rise of the automobile. New housing construction, a common indicator of economic health, also tapered off between 1925 and 1929. Four industries that employed thousands of workers slowing down was a warning sign that the boom that the American economy was experiencing may have been approaching an end.

However, other industries, especially the nascent auto industry, were booming. The conversion from a wartime economy to a more consumer-centered economy created a great amount of growth. People were buying many new and novel products that American manufacturers were all too happy to keep producing. The aforementioned automobiles were continually setting new records for sales. Other household products like refrigerators, radios, and clothes washers were new to Americans, and many were glad to have these modern conveniences.

In order to get these new products, more people than ever before were buying goods on credit. Unlike in previous generations, carrying personal debt wasn't seen as a particular danger. There was a great deal of confidence that the economy, and most importantly jobs, would continue to be plentiful. As major industries started to slow down, the use of credit also slowed. By the later part of the decade, household spending was reduced significantly, particularly because even while profits were still strong for corporations, wages rose insignificantly. Production of consumer goods didn't slow down at the same rate, and like farming, a surplus was being produced by the end of the decade. However, with less money to spend and less willingness to use credit, the high production was unsustainable in the long run.

The use of credit was also a major factor in the growth of another part of the economy, the stock market. Prior to the 1920s, the market was largely the providence of the upper class. In the 1920s, middle-class Americans began investing. For many, making an investment required more money than was on hand. The practice of buying on margin, where one purchases stock with a certain percentage of the money coming from a loan, was used by smaller investors to get in on the market. An investor could make a purchase with as much as 70 percent borrowed money, or 70 percent on margin. If the investment went up, the margin would be paid back, with the rest of the return going to the buyer. If the investment didn't rise, not only was the personal stake lost, but the borrowed money as well, which still needed to be repaid.

Adding to the spread of participation in the market was the practice of speculating. For many new investors, there was little research being done about the companies where the money was invested. Like real estate speculation in the nineteenth century, where buyers often didn't even know the location of the land they were buying, new investors knew little about the companies they were financing. Such high-risk investments were fine if the market continued to rise, but if the market slowed, or worse plunged, a lot of people would be out of a lot of money.

The volatility of the market in the fall of 1929 was troubling to a greater amount of people than it ever had been. The exclusive domain of brokers and investment bankers had now become the concern of the middle class. The banks that loaned the money for margin buys also were more concerned with the behavior of the market than they had been in previous generations. It would only take one particularly bad downswing to cause a great deal of hardship for a lot of Americans.

When Herbert Hoover was inaugurated in March of 1929, he expressed optimism for the future of the nation. The economy was steadily rising, and there was no need to worry about things going south. By the end of the year, it was apparent that something was seriously wrong with the stock market and with the economy as a whole.

The downturn that was even expected by some economists started on Thursday, October 24. However, as a great sell-off got underway, investors were worried that the market was going to fall too far. In order to pre-empt a sharp decline, JP Morgan infused a great deal of money into the market. The ploy seemed to work. After Morgan's influx of cash, the market stabilized.

However, it was only a temporary fix. The following day the market closed down again, but Morgan was not able to bail it out this time. The weekend offered some respite, but Monday saw another downturn. Tuesday, October 29, 1929, saw the greatest amount of stock traded in the history of the stock market. The loss of volume was staggering. Brokers were selling at massive discounts in hopes of salvaging some money. In the end, it just made the matter worse. The more people were selling at a loss, the more other investors wanted to get out of a bad situation. By the end of the day, known as Black Tuesday, the market was down almost 14,000 points. It was the greatest (and still is by percentage) loss in the history of Wall Street.

Black Tuesday caused great tremors throughout the economy and society, but people and institutions weren't panicking just yet. The ripples needed time to expand. First, those that had been buying on margin were in a tough situation, needing to pay back their loans. Suffering great losses made paying back the loans extremely difficult, if not impossible. Without the return of borrowed money, banks began to feel the pinch and remaining solvent for day-to-day activities became an issue. Some banks were forced to close because of the shortfall. As news and rumors swirled about the health of the banking industry, more and more people lost faith in their respective banks and started to withdraw their money. It was a destructive cycle. The more people that ran to the banks, wanting their money they thought was safe, caused more banks to fail. By 1932, more than 5,000 banks had failed.

The run on the banks accelerated the downward spiral of the economy. Spending had already been slower, but now with entire life savings wiped out, discretionary spending was all but non-existent. Businesses were starting to lay off large amounts of workers to try and reduce the corporate losses they were beginning to see. While businesses were laying people off, they were also cutting wages and hours. What many believed was just a more violent correction to the economy than usual was now seen as a significant downturn. As unemployment began to rise, meeting household expenses became a pressing concern for many families. Under such harsh circumstances, people needed assistance from outside sources. They turned to benevolent societies, churches, neighborhood organizations, and government agencies. As the crisis deepened, citizens called on the government to do more. The response to those calls defined much of the presidency of Herbert Hoover.

Chapter 2: Herbert Hoover and the Early Years of the Depression

Herbert Hoover's name is synonymous with failure. It was during his presidency that the worst economic crisis in American history occurred. Fair or not, Hoover was judged harshly by his contemporaries and by later generations. Even though many of the causes of the Great Depression were years in the making, Hoover was left holding the bag. It didn't help that the solutions he and his administration offered either didn't work or completely backfired. Oftentimes, the treatment by the federal government of those that were in desperate need was seen as cold, uncaring, and even cruel.

It is this description, of being uncaring, that is possibly the most unfair one leveled at Hoover. He came from a humble background, growing up poor in the Midwest. He was also a very religious man who believed strongly in the previous generation's progressive ethos of being helpful to his fellow citizens. His progressivism was of the Republican variety, and, like Roosevelt and Taft, he still saw it as a goal to uplift people. He famously said in 1928 that within a decade poverty could be eliminated from the United States.

After a visit to post-war Germany, Hoover was instrumental in getting an allied blockade around Germany lifted and getting much-needed food to the people of that nation. Hoover believed in aiding others, even former enemies, if the need was great and beyond the ability of those suffering. He also believed just as strongly that offering too much help was morally wrong. Pulling oneself up by the bootstraps was far better than being given a handout. Instilling or reaffirming confidence was far better than simple charity.

Such an ethos had served Hoover well in his rise to the presidency. In his youth, Hoover witnessed when things got difficult, people helping other people, communities taking care of one another. Hoover was certain that such community engagement would buoy people struggling during the current crisis. Unfortunately, when the majority of people are suffering or barely getting by, personal charity isn't realistic. Furthermore, institutions that had often provided a   social safety net in the past were completely overwhelmed. Churches, benevolent societies, unions, and other community organizations simply didn't have the resources to meet the demand of people seeking aid.

Like other presidents, Hoover tried to appeal to the consciences of business leaders. Hoover asked many captains of industry to pledge to not reduce wages or lay off any workers during the economic crisis. Many corporations agreed, but as the economic picture continued to darken, they could not (or would not) honor the pledge. Reducing labor costs to cut losses and stay in business was one of the oldest strategies and had been prevalent for 50 years prior. Such ingrained thinking wasn't going to be totally abandoned, pledge or no pledge. By 1932, between 25-30 percent of Americans were out of work. Couple that number with the amount of people who were underemployed or working intermittently and the picture becomes even starker. It is tragic, though not surprising, that in the first years of the Depression the national suicide rate rose by 30 percent.

Another strategy of the past was the implementation of higher tariffs. In 1930, with an eye toward protecting American businesses and

American workers, the Harley-Smoot Act was passed. The thinking was that with higher costs on foreign goods, people would buy more American goods, helping to boost the economy. It backfired. People didn't begin to buy in greater numbers, and other nations retaliated with tariffs of their own, hurting American businesses and causing more layoffs.

Along with the self-help ethos and sparingly delivered aid to those in need, another standard that Hoover believed in was maintaining a balanced federal budget. Deficit spending was only permissible in times of war. Domestic strife was not the time to panic and take drastic actions and possibly make things worse overall. As some federal dollars were trickling out to help people deal with the Depression, Hoover proposed a tax increase to maintain the balanced budget. Even though the president's political party was in control of Congress, they did not support Hoover's plan to increase taxes.

Despite his best efforts, Hoover could not stem the tide of the rising economic crisis. Even more, circumstances beyond his control made matters worse for the nation and for the public's perception of the president. Some of the hardest hit states made up the world's breadbasket, and from the Dakotas to Texas, a severe drought in the 1930s made farming there almost impossible. The topsoil across the entire region was so dry that the wind would pick it up and cause near blackout conditions, creating what contemporaries called the Dust Bowl. When the winds stopped blowing, massive drifts of soil covered farming equipment, rose against farm buildings, and made thousands of farms untenable. Though an act of nature, the lack of response by the president added to the perception that he was out of touch or didn't care about average Americans. The slow and perceived lack of response tainted Hoover's legacy.

As the Dust Bowl shifted and moved the soil across the plains, the economic hardships of the Depression caused great displacement among people throughout the United States. Those that were turned out of their homes had little recourse except to create the best shelter that they could. Many families were forced to create makeshift tents or lean-tos in order to provide some shelter. These shanty towns sprang up in every major city in the United States. Though there was little that Hoover could have done, these vagabond settlements became known as Hoovervilles, with the implication being that he was personally at fault.

While the Dust Bowl and Hoovervilles were well beyond Hoover's control, one event that he could have prevented was a public relations nightmare for the president. In 1929, before the Depression started, Congress passed and Hoover signed a bill establishing a monetary bonus for surviving World War I veterans. The payments weren't scheduled to begin until 1945.

When it became apparent that the Depression wasn't a short-term event, the veterans wanted their promised bonuses to come early to help during the present crisis. In order to pressure Congress to act, thousands of veterans camped out on the National Mall in 1932 and expressed their desire to be paid immediately. After a number of days, this "Bonus Army" moved to another section of Washington, DC. At no time were the former soldiers violent, or even threatening violence. However, after a week of protesting simply by their presence, Hoover ordered the active army to clear the veterans from the capital. A cavalry regiment, along with a tank, were sent out to disperse the vets. Under the command of Douglas MacArthur and including other future famous generals such as George Patton and Dwight Eisenhower, the army horsemen rode down the former soldiers. Numerous were injured and two men were killed in the action.

There are very few untouchables in American politics, but military veterans are among them. Since the beginning of the country, former soldiers hold a special place in the national conscience. Even the Bonus Army, made up of those that fought for the nation, was to be respected and honored, not attacked. The public reaction to the event was profoundly negative for Hoover. Even before the Bonus Army episode, Hoover was becoming more and more withdrawn from the public view. After the conflict, Hoover was almost completely out of the public view. He felt that he was being attacked from all sides and remaining out of sight offered him some respite. This was also in keeping with the common attitude of many former presidents. It wasn't the president's job to be present all of the time, to be a public face. Presidents were supposed to be aloof, guarded. As the election of 1932 approached, Hoover was going to run again. Little did he realize that his opponent would change what was expected of a president and define the office for decades to come.

Chapter 3: The Election of 1932

The election of 1928 was one of the most revealing elections for the United States. It demonstrated the power of the urban, ethnic working class and also the deep prejudices that the country still held, especially toward Catholics. Herbert Hoover ran on his past accomplishments in federal government and on the success of his party in the post-war world. The Republican Party also engaged in personal attacks on the Democratic nominee. Al Smith, the Democratic nominee and governor of New York, was a Roman Catholic. The fear of being controlled by the pope and the practice of a very foreign religion for many Americans was capitalized on by Hoover and the Republicans. They claimed that they were fighting to protect the nation from foreign control. In addition, Smith was a "wet," an advocate of repealing prohibition. This combination of a Catholic who supported repeal was too much for the majority of Americans. Even though Prohibition was unpopular, many Americans still saw it as an important way to protect society.

Hoover won the presidency handily in 1928, but he faced a much different electorate in 1932. The economy was approaching the nadir of the Depression. It appeared that Hoover wasn't doing anything to make things better for average Americans. The Republican Party was at the wheel for all of the downfall and was seen as responsible for the current situation. Finally, the great issues that had turned many voters against Al Smith would not be present with the new candidate in 1932.

The new candidate was a part of New York politics and part of one of the most iconic American families. Unlike his elder cousin, Theodore, Franklin Delano made his way for the Democratic Party, not the Republican. He was part of the Wilson administration, and like Al Smith, he was a former governor of New York. Due to late-onset polio when he was in his late thirties, his mobility was limited by the use of a wheelchair.

In many ways, given the backgrounds of the candidates, one might assume Hoover was the Democrat and Roosevelt the Republican. Not only because of the family history with the Grand Old Party, but the Roosevelt family was also one of the first Dutch families to settle in New Amsterdam. By the dawn of Franklin's generation, the family was quite accustomed to wealth and privilege. While both sides of the family believed in the concept of noblesse oblige, Franklin thought it was just as important to use government to better society than to simply serve the people. He harkened back to the activist progressives of the earlier part of the century. Many of his peers considered Roosevelt a traitor to his class.

Two of the main wedge issues that Hoover used against Smith did not work against Roosevelt. Roosevelt was firmly in the American Protestant tradition, so the division by religion was muted. The other issue that was divisive in 1928, prohibition, had almost completely swung toward the position Smith held. By 1932, much of the nation viewed prohibition as a failed experiment. Roosevelt, himself was known to enjoy a cocktail from time to time, even asked during speeches, "Shouldn't a man be able to enjoy a beer after a hard day's labor?" For many Americans, the answer was yes.

Instead of trying to paint their opponent as an outsider harboring a dangerous religion and destructive social behavior, Hoover and the

Republicans portrayed Roosevelt as an out of touch dandy who was going to spend the nation's money carelessly. Under Roosevelt, the national debt would rise, businesses would suffer, and the depression would only worsen.

Roosevelt countered by portraying Hoover as a do-nothing president. He wasn't only uncaring, the Democrats insisted, but unwilling to do anything to help the majority of Americans. The Democrats laid the blame for the Great Depression at the feet of Herbert Hoover and the Republicans in control of Congress. The decision voters faced was between something new or the status quo; at least, it was how the Democrats posed the question.

The candidate Roosevelt wasn't the only new aspect of the Democratic campaign. While he stumped across the country, Roosevelt and many other Democrats promised a "New Deal" for all Americans. The name stuck and was the overarching name for Roosevelt's legislative agenda going forward. It also became a term for those that enacted the agenda, the New Dealers. The term was also the name given to the coalition of voters that Roosevelt was able to knit together for elections for almost twenty years.

The New Deal was more than a catchy name. Roosevelt promised industrial recovery, agricultural recovery, and short-term relief for the jobless. These promises resonated with voters from a broad spectrum of the electorate. The promise of industrial recovery and a reputation for being pro-union attracted the urban, ethnic working class. Promising to focus on agricultural recovery attracted voters from the Midwest and the South. Without the handicap of Catholicism, the Dixiecrats (Democrats for the states that formed the Confederacy in the Civil War) were much more willing to vote for their party's national nominee. Perhaps the most remarkable aspect of the New Deal Coalition was the inclusion of African Americans to the Democratic Party. The election of 1932 saw for the first time that the majority of African Americans voted for a Democratic candidate. Long seen as the party of slavery and racism, the Democrats were able to enhance their appeal to African Americans who were no longer in the South. Instead, African Americans were a much greater part of the urban centers of the United States due to the Great Migration that started during World War I and continued through the 1920s. Once a solid block of voters for the party of Lincoln, African Americans opted for change.

The rest of the nation felt the same way. By a margin of 57 percent to 39 percent, Roosevelt defeated Herbert Hoover. The margin was even greater when looking at the electoral college results. Roosevelt carried 472 electoral votes to Hoover's 59. Hoover was only able to hold 6 states to Roosevelt's 42. It wasn't just the presidential election either. For the first time in over a decade, the Democratic Party gained majorities in the House of Representatives and the Senate. Americans were ready for a change. They were ready for a new deal.

Chapter 4: The 100 Days and FDR's First Term, 1933-1937

Franklin Delano Roosevelt was sworn in as the thirty-second president of the United States on March 19, 1933. He used the occasion to inspire the nation and projected confidence in the nation that too few actually felt. He said one of the most famous lines ever spoken by a president, "The only thing we have to fear, is fear itself." It is interesting to note that the new president said, we, not you. Roosevelt wanted it to be clear that he was a part of the struggle, and that he was going to work at ending the Depression right along with everyone else. The work started right away. By midsummer, the first 100 days of Roosevelt's first term were complete. Ever since 1933, every first term of a president is judged on that same scale, 100 days.

The flurry of activity that the new administration engaged in was staggering. Roosevelt summed up the philosophy of such an approach by saying, "We are going to try new things. If those don't work, we are going to try something else. No matter we will keep trying until something works." New departments were set up on what seemed like a daily basis. Legislative initiatives from the White

House and Congress were constantly being debated and approved. Not all of the proposals worked, as Roosevelt predicted, but he was not going to be considered a do-nothing president from the first day.

Some key policies were enacted in the first 100 days. One of the first was the Emergency Banking Act. A mandatory bank holiday was declared. With all of the banks closed, the federal government assessed which banks were healthy, which could be saved, and which were too far gone and needed to be closed permanently. The banks that could be saved were brought under the management of the government. The eventual goal of the program was to restore faith in the banks and help bolster the economy.

Further reaffirming consumer faith in the banking system was the creation of the Federal Deposit Insurance Corporation. This new government-controlled corporation guaranteed deposits up to $100,000 in the event of the bank's closure. Until the Great Depression, there was no such assurance. Though banks were often seen as safe places to keep money, for that entire generation living through the Depression, even with the FDIC, banks were suspect. Still, the new agency helped to fulfill one of the key campaign promises of Roosevelt and the Democrats, revitalizing the economy.

Another key provision of the New Deal platform was short-term relief for the jobless. To that end, the Roosevelt administration created the Civilian Conservation Corps. The CCC was a program to employ single young men at the onset but later expanded to a greater portion of the population. The enrollees were sent to camps within areas of the United States that needed conservation work, by stopping soil erosion, constructing fire towers, planting trees, and a host of other tasks. By the end of its first year, 1933, the CCC employed over 250,000 men. The program was a success and very popular. It did not solve all of the employment problems facing the United States, but it helped both financially and psychologically. A great number of workers felt useful again. It also further demonstrated that Roosevelt was taking action.

Along those same lines, the Federal Emergency Relief Act established the Federal Emergency Relief Administration. FERA was created in 1933, like the CCC. Instead of being a strictly federal agency, FERA distributed $500 million to state and local agencies to help the unemployed. Many of the jobs created were unskilled labor, but like the jobs at the CCC, they provided a morale boost to those that were out of work.

The most ambitious employment act undertaken was the establishment of the Works Progress Administration. This initiative employed thousands in its first year of existence and reached millions at its peak later in the decade. Many of the buildings and projects constructed under the direction of the WPA are now historically preserved sites. Thousands of schools, post offices, bridges, and hospitals were constructed during the 1930s boom of the WPA. Over 625,000 miles of roads were laid by the organization. It was the greatest expansion of infrastructure ever in the United States.

The construction projects were the greater part of the WPA, but another initiative of the program was specifically directed toward helping unemployed artists. Federal Project Number One was composed of five key parts: the Federal Writers Project, the Federal Theatre Project, the Federal Arts Project, the Federal Music Project, and the Historical Records Project. Thousands of writers, actors, and musicians were employed by the government, creating pamphlets, posters, guides to national parks, and a host of other projects. Many well-known and later successful artists took part in the program including Orson Welles, Burt Lancaster, and Sidney Lumet. One of the most important projects from the WPA was the collection of American slave narratives. The stories of over 2,000 slaves were recorded and preserved, maintaining an important link to one of the most tragic aspects of American history.

Agricultural recovery was another key component of the 1932 platform. To that end, the Roosevelt administration proposed the Agricultural Adjustment Act which, when passed, created the

Agricultural Adjustment Administration. The main purpose of this new agency was to help farmers with surpluses and to reduce the amount of food being produced. The government bought and slaughtered surplus livestock and paid farmers not to plant crops that were running surpluses and were not in high demand. For tenant farmers and sharecroppers, the AAA was a bit of a mixed bag. While the landowners were paid not to produce on a portion of their land, those tenants and croppers were all but cut out of the surplus payments. However, many owners allowed the tenants and croppers to stay on the land and plant their own crops. This led to more food for tenants and also allowed them to bring their own crops to market. While the amount of money wasn't large, it helped to raise the standard of living of many tenant farmers and sharecroppers.

Though not strictly a measure for the agricultural sector of the economy, the Tennessee Valley Authority, created in 1933, benefited some of the most remote and underdeveloped areas of the United States. The TVA brought modernization to most of Tennessee, parts of Alabama, Kentucky, Mississippi, Georgia, North Carolina, and Virginia. The Authority built dams, produced fertilizer, and provided electricity throughout the region. In addition to providing such services, the TVA employed thousands in order to deliver those services to the region. The organization is still owned and operated by the federal government.

The most controversial aspect of the first 100 days was the legislation proposed to help industry recover, another key tenant of the campaign trail. The National Industry Recovery Act (NIRA) was eventually passed by the House and Senate but not without a great deal of opposition. The legislation eventually created the National Recovery Administration (NRA) and the Public Works Administration (PWA). The acts' intent was to provide workers with protections they did not currently enjoy, such as allowing collective bargaining and banning the practice of coercing employees to not join a union or engage in a union activity. The act also tried to enforce fair competition and regulated other aspects of various industries. Ultimately, that was where a great deal of criticism for the act was aimed. The NRA produced hundreds of new regulations, seemingly overnight. Many allies of Roosevelt turned against the administration over the NRA, and business leaders especially did not like what they felt to be government overreach.

Though not necessarily a campaign promise, one of the main concerns of many Americans was pulling in the reigns of Wall Street, the entity many blamed for the financial collapse in the first place. The Securities Act of 1933 was the key part of that initiative. The act eventually led to the creation of the Securities and Exchange Commission. It was the first federal legislation to regulate the trade of stocks in the United States. The main thrust of the legislation was to put a curb on speculative buying by requiring tighter disclosures on the terms of a particular sale. In short, all of the risk that an investment might carry needed to be part of any sale that used interstate commerce. The act also provided any investor who was defrauded the avenue to sue the issuer of the sale.

During the first 100 days, Roosevelt also started a regular feature of his presidency that, like the 100-day benchmark, became the standard for future presidents. Each week, Roosevelt did a weekly update on the initiatives that the government was enacting. He also offered words of encouragement to Americans about their current situation and assured them he was doing all he could to turn the country around. These "Fireside Chats" were amazingly successful. Radio was still a relatively new medium for many Americans and such direct contact from the president was unheard of before. Many survivors of the Great Depression remembered listening as a family to the radio to hear what the president, their president, had to say.

The flurry of activity of these 100 days has never been matched by another incoming president. The amount of major legislation reaching various sectors of American life proved to the people of the United States that the new president wasn't all talk. He was good to his campaign word. Not everything worked, but like Roosevelt said, they were willing to try and try again. The financial sector, unemployment, and rural areas all benefited from the first round of legislation within the New Deal. Two other major pieces of legislation came during Roosevelt's first term. Both were cornerstones of the New Deal policy and both are still in effect today. The first dealt with people who were employed and the second for people who have finished working or can no longer work.

The National Labor Relations Act (NLRA), also known as the Wagner Act, established the National Labor Relations Board (NLRB) and provided federal safeguards for collective bargaining, unionizing, and striking. The act defined and tried to stop unfair labor practices, and included protections for employees who testify against their employer in criminal or civil court. The act did not cover workers employed by the railways or working in the federal government. In order to appease Southern lawmakers, domestic workers and agricultural workers were also excluded from the protections of the Wagner Act. These two professions were singled out because the majority of domestic workers and agricultural workers in the South were African Americans.

The other monumental piece of legislation passed in 1935 was the Social Security Act. This act provided former employees a stipend after they had worked, made provisions for unemployment, gave aid to families with dependent children, had provisions for maternal and child welfare, provided for public health, and provided assistance to the blind. It was one of the most ambitious policies ever enacted by the United States government. Until the advent of Social Security, American workers often needed to remain employed well into their advanced age. Often, employees worked until they quite simply couldn't work any longer. If they were lucky, there were savings available, but especially in the Depression with bank closings, that was less likely. In order to pass the legislation, like the NLRA, domestic and agricultural workers were excluded from the legislation.

In both cases, the NLRA and the Social Security Act, the Republican Party and various business groups vehemently opposed the efforts.

In the case of the NLRA, employers were especially critical of the Relations Board pro-union bias. While the idea was to be an impartial judge in labor disputes, the NLRB did seem to lean more toward employees than employers. In the case of Social Security, the main criticism was that the program was simply socialism under a different name. Most conservatives in Congress voiced such concerns and voted accordingly, though the bill still passed.

As FDR's first term came to an end, it was hard not to see it as a success, at least as far as enacting an agenda on the national stage. How successful the programs were was a bit more muddled of a picture. Hundreds of thousands were given work, albeit sometimes only temporarily, and people, especially the elderly, were brought back from the brink of great suffering. Programs were enacted to help both urban and rural people, and something resembling confidence was being shown toward the financial sector of the economy. Unemployment, however, remained stubbornly high. Businesses were still not able to bring workers back in large part because people were still unable to buy goods at pre-Depression rates. The situation may have felt better and even looked better, but there was still a long way to go.

Chapter 5: FDR's Second Term— Challenges and Critics

Though no election is a sure thing, in 1936 there was little doubt that Franklin Roosevelt would win a second term. The economy was still struggling, but it was on the upswing. More importantly, the majority of Americans approved of the job Roosevelt was doing. They believed that the aristocrat from New York was the best choice to lead the nation out of the worst economic disaster in the country's history.

The Republican challenger was the governor of Kansas, Alf Landon, who famously remarked during the campaign, "Everywhere I go I see Americans." Obvious observations aside, it is a wonder if Landon actually saw anyone during the campaign. He rarely traveled outside of his home state, while Roosevelt was engaged throughout the campaign season, traveling across the country. Though there was some discussion that it could be a close race, even the most ardent Republican could have predicted the results. Roosevelt won in a landslide, capturing 60 percent of the popular vote, carrying 46 of the 48 states, and capturing 523 of a possible 531 electoral votes. It remains one of the largest margins of victory ever. Along with Roosevelt's crushing victory, the Democrats took even more seats in Congress.

With such a mandate, Roosevelt and Congress were ready to enact further aspects of the New Deal. Unfortunately for FDR, much of his second term was occupied with his dealings with the Supreme Court. According to Roosevelt and his allies, the court was the one stumbling block to keeping the New Deal intact. Starting in 1935, a string of court cases went against Roosevelt and New Deal initiatives. The most notable reverses were against the National Industrial Recovery Act and the Agricultural Adjustment Act. Leading the charge on the court, headed by Chief Justice Charles Evans Hughes, were four conservative justices, later coined the "Four Horsemen." These justices, Pierce Butler, James Clark McReynolds, George Sutherland, and Willis Van Devanter, respectively were seen as the largest opponents of the New Deal. Three of the four were appointed by Republican presidents. The fourth, McReynolds, was appointed by Woodrow Wilson, but was a conservative Southerner. The first case, *Panama Refining Company v. Ryan*, declared that the National Industrial Recovery Act restriction on interstate and international trade of petroleum surpluses was unconstitutional. Chief Justice Hughes wrote the majority opinion and ruled that specific parameters needed to be set in such cases and not at the discretion of the executive branch. In sum, it was a check on Roosevelt's power.

The court went even further against the NIRA in the *Schechter Poultry Corp. v. United States* case. In the unanimous decision, also written by Chief Justice Hughes, the NIRA legislation granted powers to the executive branch that were enumerated for the legislative branch of the government. More damning was the ruling that even the provisions within the law that were within the power of Congress violated the Commerce Clause, which gave Congress the power, albeit limited power, to regulate trade within states.

Another signature piece of the New Deal was declared unconstitutional the following year in 1936. The court ruled in *United States v. Butler* that the Agricultural Adjustment Act violated the Constitution by levying an unfair tax on food producers and went beyond the scope of national government power by regulating how much a farmer could grow. Between 1934 and 1936, of the 16 cases pertaining to New Deal legislation, 10 went against Roosevelt and the New Deal.

In 1937, after his reelection, Roosevelt tried to pass legislation that would tilt the court in his favor. He noted that there was no specific law or requirement that the Supreme Court be made up of nine members. There were various iterations of the number on the court, but by 1869, nine was the established number. Roosevelt tried to "pack" the court with nominees of his choosing in order to protect New Deal programs. The plan called for the president to nominate a justice for every justice over the age of 70. The president was limited to six such appointments, but could conceivably gain six favorable seats on a court of fifteen potential members. Roosevelt brought his idea to the public during one of his Fireside Chats. He argued that the court was out of touch with reality and with the Constitution. He further argued that his plan was needed to save the New Deal, save the nation, and save the Supreme Court itself.

Reaction was swift and largely negative. Republicans and conservatives saw it as an unprecedented power grab. Many Democrats felt the same way and went public with their feelings. The public was very much against the idea as well. Unlike so many of Roosevelt's proposals and ideas, the plan to pack the court met with only a minority of support from voters. A massive letter writing campaign was launched opposing the bill. It was easily the largest and most costly error of Roosevelt's presidency. It turned many former allies against the administration in Congress, and public opinion of the president suffered as well.

What is ironic in the case of court packing were two events. First the Panama case and Schechter case were unanimous rulings, 9-0. Even with six friendly judges, both still would have been losses for the president. The second event was that Justice Van Devanter, one of the Four Horsemen, retired in 1937. Roosevelt was now presented with appointing a justice, making the "liberal" wing four, the "conservative" three, with two swing voters. As Roosevelt's presidency continued, he would appoint nine justices to the court. More than any other president, Roosevelt shaped the direction of American law for decades by appointing more justices than anyone else. In the end, Roosevelt didn't need a scheme to tilt the court in his favor, just time.

The court-packing controversy saw a great deal of criticism directed at President Roosevelt, but this wasn't the first time he had faced critics. Two, in particular, a demagogue and a Catholic priest, were particularly vocal about the president. They both had considerable followings and considerable platforms to get their anti-Roosevelt message to the public. One hailed from the Deep South, the other from the industrial Midwest, specifically Detroit, Michigan. Huey Long and Father Charles Coughlin weren't the only critics of Roosevelt but were perhaps the most widely known. Both started out as supporters of the New Deal, but soon soured on the program and its architect.

Huey Long was a politician from Louisiana who was known as "The Kingfish" in his native state. Though the name was taken from the famous radio show, "Amos 'n' Andy," there was very little that was humorous about Long and his hold on Louisiana politics. After winning the governorship in 1928, Long consolidated his power by removing any and everyone in the government that stood in opposition to him. He built an enormous patronage system that made practically everyone working in state government loyal to him. Long was not popular with the landed-elite, but in the rest of the state, he was unopposed.

Long was a vehement critic of big business and the financial system of the United States. Much of his policies in Louisiana reflected the same ideals that would define the New Deal in 1933. Long, an elected senator from Louisiana in 1932, was a vocal supporter of Roosevelt and the New Deal. Perhaps he was too vocal. Roosevelt appreciated the help, but also distanced himself from the populist from the South. When the National Industrial Recovery Act was proposed, Long believed that is was too soft on employers and corporations.

Roosevelt all but cut Long out from New Deal strategy and referred to him as "one of the most dangerous men in America." Long continued to be an outspoken critic of American businesses and elites and proposed a new program, "Share Our Wealth," which would limit personal fortunes and redistribute wealth to every American. Not gaining many allies in Congress, Long turned to the people and started the Share Our Wealth Society. By 1935, there were over 7 million members with 27,000 local chapters. Long often reached radio audiences over 25 million strong with his message of wealth distribution.

It is debated whether or not Long was eyeing a presidential run in 1936, but it wasn't out of the realm of possibility. He had a strong base of support, a national platform, and a campaigning ability that was second to none, including Roosevelt. He even had substantial allies both inside and outside of politics. Unfortunately for Huey Long and the Share Our Wealth Society, he had a lot of enemies. One of those enemies, more specifically the son-in-law of one of those enemies, shot and killed Huey Long in September of 1935.

One of Long's allies, and critic of Roosevelt, was Father Charles Coughlin. He was a parish priest in suburban Detroit and began his radio career speaking out against the Ku Klux Klan which was operating in Michigan at the time. His anti-Klan stance and style attracted CBS, and they began to broadcast his show nationally.

With the advent of the Depression, Coughlin spoke more and more about political and economic issues and the need for the national government to do more. With the election of 1932 and the rise of Roosevelt and the New Deal, Coughlin thought his prayers had been answered.

By 1934, like Huey Long, Father Coughlin was disillusioned with Roosevelt and what he considered the slow pace of the New Deal. Coughlin also felt that the president was going beyond the Constitution and was too enamored with capitalism to be truly effective. The priest founded the National Union for Social Justice (NUSJ), which was dedicated to wealth redistribution, nationalizing certain industries, and reforming the entire financial system. The NUSJ and Coughlin were particularly critical of banks and the Federal Reserve System, which he felt was mostly responsible for the Depression.

As the decade continued, Coughlin still had strong support among his listeners. That was about to change, however. As early as 1936, Coughlin started expressing anti-Semitic views and sharing conspiracy theories about Jewish control of the economy. He was continually linked to fascists in Europe, and while Coughlin tried to distance himself from pro-fascist groups in the United States, he sometimes defended Nazi actions. When World War II broke out in Europe, Coughlin was a staunch isolationist. When the United States entered the war in 1941, Coughlin still remained opposed to US involvement. His opposition was seen as sympathetic to the enemy, and steps were started to take him off the air and tried for sedition. The Catholic hierarchy, however, stepped in and ordered Coughlin to end his show and return to being simply a parish priest. In the end, that is what Coughlin did, remaining as a pastor until his retirement in 1966.

Chapter 6: The Culture of the Depression

The Great Depression spawned a number of cultural movements in the United States. Many associate the decade of the Depression with radicalism and political culture. Many artists joined political parties, especially the Communist Party, and expressed their politics in their writings, artwork, films, and plays. Even those that didn't join political movements were influenced by current events.

Though the Communist Party saw its greatest growth during the Great Depression, there was another, less organized aspect of 1930s culture that was equally profound. Many Americans looked to the nation's past for a remedy to the current situation. The idea of discovering what it meant to be an American, what was the American way of life, was a question many tried to answer.

In both approaches, that of radicalism and traditionalism, the overriding theme of the cultural landscape of the Depression was one of coping with hard times. Americans found a way through various media (radio, film, and music to name a few) to find a way of dealing with the harsh realities of the day. Not all of these outlets were just concerned with the New Deal and current events. There were many means of entertainment that were designed to simply help people forget for a while. Escapism was especially helpful to many throughout the era and just as important as other works. Mickey Mouse and Dorothy from *The Wizard of Oz* had just as significant a role in the culture of the 1930s as the Popular Front and the works of John Steinbeck.

Though the medium of radio was already popular in the 1920s, the 1930s was perhaps the golden age of radio. By the 1930s, all of the nation's Major League Baseball teams had broadcasts. There were many cultural and educational programs, including broadcasts of opera and informational programing. The most popular broadcasts, however, were the variety shows and soap operas. The variety hours were reminiscent of vaudeville shows that once traveled across the country. Musical acts, comical skits, and other performances all made their way into family living rooms on a nightly basis.

The soap opera was the programming that dominated the airwaves though. Shows like *The Goldbergs*, which highlighted the lives of an immigrant family living in New York, gained millions of listeners. For many Americans, they could either remember similar circumstances or had family members who lived such events. People identified with the characters and wanted to know what would happen next. Other programs followed a similar formula, all designed to keep people tuned in. Some shows, such as *XXXX*, contained more melodrama and highlighted an almost fantasy life of wealth and fame, but it still kept audiences coming back. A day of hard work, or worse no work, was made better by the familiar rhythms of the serialized drama.

Familiar rhythms were a key to another avenue of entertainment throughout the decade, music. The 1920s saw the advent of jazz as the popular music of the time, but the music of the 1930s expanded on the ideas of jazz and became a bigger sound. Swing music was the music of the 1930s. Big bands played a more dance-friendly style of music, and though money was tight, people still flocked to see, listen, and most importantly dance to new music as often as they could. Dance halls enticed people to come to their places by running contests called dance marathons. Couples would dance until there was only one couple left on the floor. They were the winner and usually won a cash prize. It may not have been the best way to make a living, but it was surely a fun way to earn some extra money on the weekend.

The motion picture industry of the 1930s had aspects of all of these cultural threads, escapism, radicalism, and a search for tradition. In the case of escapism, no company is a better example than Walt Disney Studios. Disney's first success came from the creation of the character that has remained a symbol of the company, Mickey Mouse. First in black and white and then in color, Mickey Mouse short films were extremely popular. But Walt Disney wanted animation to do more, be more. In 1937, the Walt Disney Company produced its first full-length feature, *Snow White and the Seven Dwarves*. It was an instant success. Audiences fell in love with the story, and it was the top grossing movie in 1938. *The Wizard of Oz* from 1939 was also a wonderfully escapist film, with the central idea of recovery, of being safe.

Another genre of film that was enormously popular in the 1930s and was part of the escapist tradition of cinema were monster films. Universal Studios in particular became known for the cast of monster films they produced, including *Frankenstein* (1931), *Dracula* (1931), *The Mummy* (1932), and *The Invisible Man* (1933). All of these movies revolved around similar plots, a great supernatural threat, and the heroes working together to save the world. It was a reassuring message in an otherwise uncertain time. None of these films, however, captured the imagination like *King Kong* (1933), the film some still consider the best horror movie of all time.

Not all of Hollywood's output was strictly of an escapist nature. Many films of the period included social commentary. Obvious messages like in *Robin Hood* (1938) highlighted the concept of wealth redistribution and the upper classes being the enemy of the people. The concept of the power of the everyman was also explored in films like *Mr. Smith Goes to Washington* (1939). Other films, such as *Duck Soup* (1933), contained social commentary about international tensions of the period, and *Modern Times* (1936) starring Charlie Chaplin was a critique of the impersonal nature of the industrial workplace and economy. No series of films or film stars expressed the ethos of the New Deal better than Will Rogers.

Calling himself the "#1 New Dealer," Will Rogers' public persona and popular films had a blend of populism, radical traditionalism, and the redistribution of wealth contained in the stories. The 1930s audience had lost faith in the wealthy and political leaders, but the characters portrayed by Rogers in twenty-four different films reaffirmed the place and power of the community. The lead characters stop putting their faith in Wall Street and corporations and instead put their faith in Americanism. Rogers, the person not the character, brought legitimacy to the message by being deeply rooted in the history of the United States, especially those that were historically marginalized. Rogers was quoted as saying, "My people didn't come over here on the Mayflower," alluding to the fact that he grew up on an Indian reservation in Oklahoma as a part of the Cherokee Nation. His embrace and celebration of what it meant to be an American carried more weight than others. He was more American than the white European upper class that had led the nation to its current predicament. Recent immigrants, African Americans, and lower-class whites all found resonance in the message of Will Rogers.

Will Rogers represented radical traditionalism, but there was also a trend within American culture that focused on finding meaning from the past by looking in the annals of history to see what was good about America and what could be useful for the current state of affairs. *Gone with the Wind* (1936 novel; 1939 film) was a celebration of the Antebellum South. Though the main plot was an epic love story, the theme of rising up after catastrophe was a key element of the appeal of the book and film. If Scarlett (the South) could regain her prominence after devastation, then perhaps the United States could do the same.

Similarly, the works of Laura Ingalls Wilder evoked a similar ethos. Semi-autobiographical in nature, the stories of Wilder tell the tale of a pioneering family as they made their way west in search of a better life. Through a series of adventures, confronting nature, Native Americans, and economic hardship, Wilder and her family were able to persevere and eventually prosper. Written throughout the 1930s, the "Little House" books provided a uniquely American story, one that many middle-class Americans could relate to. They saw in Wilder's story aspects of their own past. If they, like their pioneering forebears, could survive the harsh world of the American West, then perhaps they could similarly weather the storm of the Great Depression.

An overall theme in much of American culture during the Depression was a search for what was the American way of life. To this end, many traditional aspects of American culture were investigated and celebrated. Folk music was of particular interest to cultural curators such as John Lomax and his son Neil. In addition, there was a substantial interest in American folk art, such as nineteenth-century furniture making and quilting. Books, such as *American Humor: A Study in National Character* (1931) by Constance Rourke and *The Flowering of New England* (1936) by Van Wyck Brooks, tried to discover what were the underpinnings of modern America. These books and many other cultural works sought to find out what made America so great, beyond its financial, industrial, and innovative successes of the previous decade. The aspects that still survived after the Depression showed that material success could be very fleeting.

This search for the "real" America was most evident in the resurgence of religion into American life. 1934 is considered a pivotal year in the history of religion in the United States. Evangelical Protestantism saw the greatest strides during the time period. The overall message from many faiths was the establishment of the theological hierarchy that many saw as abandoned in the decade before. Further, it stressed the personal aspects of failure rather than the idea of a systemic failure within the United States. The American way of life was not at fault, but the individual had failed.

Alcoholics Anonymous, founded in 1935, is a strong example of this notion. The individual alcoholic has a problem with drinking, not all of society. In order to recover from alcoholism, the alcoholic needed to "get right with God." The group was founded by a former stockbroker, Bill Wilson, and a proctologist, Dr. Bob Smith. The two met when Wilson was on a business trip to Akron, where Smith practiced medicine. The two met and developed an approach to help the individual alcoholic through personal and group interactions. Their approach was codified in 1939 with the publication of the book, *Alcoholics Anonymous*, where the group got its name. Eventually the group spread across the United States and eventually around the world.

Similarly, the rise of the self-help books, such as *How to Win Friends and Influence People* (1936) by Dale Carnegie, was another example of the individual being at fault, not society. As the New Deal was making wholesale changes to the American economy and other more extreme voices were calling for greater changes, Carnegie emphasized working on one's personal relationships to improve not only one's current situation, but to improve society as a whole, without disruptions to the greater socio-economic structure. Another self-help author like Carnegie, Henry C. Link, published *The Return to Religion* (1936) which bridges the ideas of religion and personality enhancement. In his work, Link even developed a way to discover how effective a person was through their "personality quotient." The message was clear; having a winning personality, not systemic change, was the way out of the Depression.

Just as important to the alcoholic and religious organizations was the idea of working with others. The foundation that many sought as the

American way of life was being part of something greater, of joining, of fitting in. In AA's case that was working and meeting with other alcoholics; however, many other groups flourished during the 1930s, if not for completely altruistic or political reasons, but to simply keep busy. However, it was these commitments to others, to organizations, that became the calling card of the decade.

The concept of working with others, of joining together, was also part of a more radical agenda. It would not be fair to say that everyone that joined political organizations in the 1930s was simply doing so to keep busy until employment returned. As the Depression deepened, many intellectuals in the United States openly questioned the viability of capitalism and the western tradition of liberalism. Philosophers such as John Dewey openly questioned traditional modes of thinking about American government and the economy. They looked at the new Soviet Union and saw success. Joseph Stalin seemed to have brought order to a chaotic region of the world while the west was on the brink of collapse. As the Depression worsened under Hoover, many advocated for the abandonment of private enterprise entirely.

When Roosevelt was swept into office and the New Deal became the focal point of government action, more radical thinkers felt that the program did not go far enough. They believed that Roosevelt, himself a scion of wealth and privilege, was too tied to old Republican notions of capitalism. In their view, the New Deal was just as disorganized as capitalism itself. These radical ideas found allies in a number of artists throughout the 1930s. There was a drive to find a true working-class culture within the United States. Authors such as Upton Sinclair, Richard Wright, and James Agee demanded action from the government and society. Perhaps the best-known novel of the period was *The Grapes of Wrath* (1939) by John Steinbeck, which is one of the harshest criticisms of American society that has ever been produced.

According to historian Michael Denning in his work *The Cultural Front* (1996), the 1930s was a second American Renaissance of

American culture, largely a product of and influenced by the working class. Or, as he calls it, "the proletarianization of American culture." Much of this working-class culture was an extension of a movement emanating from the Soviet Union, referred to as the Popular Front.

Before discussing in greater detail the Popular Front and its cultural implications, a brief discussion of the Communist Party, specifically the Communist Party USA (CPUSA) is in order. The CPUSA was founded in 1919 as a split of the more left wing of the Socialist Labor Party. It was not the best time to declare a new communist party in the United States. 1919 was a very anti-communist period within the United States, culminating in the Palmer Raids and the First Red Scare. Because of the crackdown on leftist activities from the federal government, especially through the newly formed Federal Bureau of Investigation (FBI) and internecine fighting among party members, CPUSA had only about 6,000 members in 1932.

During the Great Depression, many became disillusioned with capitalism and the structure of the US government. Membership in CPUSA grew by the thousands, reaching a high point later in the decade with 55,000 members. The election of Roosevelt and the New Deal was also a boon for the CPUSA, especially after the party stopped being such a vocal opposition to FDR and Democratic policies. The CPUSA still opposed racial segregation and other racist policies of Southern Democrats, but the upsurge in union membership throughout the decade was seen as a net gain when considering the overall goal of revolution from capitalism. By the election of 1936, the CPUSA didn't openly campaign for the Democrats but did see them as the better alternative.

International developments led to a call for even greater unity among communists, classic liberals, socialists, and centrists. The rise of fascism in Europe in countries like Italy, Spain, and especially Germany made the Communist International (COMINTERN) issue a directive that all communist parties in the world should work together to defeat fascism by creating a Popular Front. Within the

United States, the Popular Front was more than just the CPUSA. There was a great deal of activity within the labor movement and also among African Americans living in Harlem.

The political goal of the Popular Front was a united global resistance to fascism. In order to carry out that goal, the Popular Front engaged in various activities, from organizing and protesting to campaigning, and especially cultural outreach. The ideal movement was a combination of proletariats, writers, artists, and intellectuals reaching out to the masses of the US population. One of the main ways to do this was to engage in agitprop, or agitation propaganda. Various artists, such as Woody Guthrie and Paul Robeson, performed various anti-fascist songs and spoke out against fascism and racial injustice.

At various points in the 1930s, the cultural activities of the Popular Front were the proletariat avant-garde, a movement culture, part of the state-sponsored culture and part of the mass culture. Young artists formed clubs and societies to promulgate new directions in leftist art. As part of the movement, many of those same artists performed for union gatherings and at demonstrations. As mentioned in an earlier chapter, many writers, actors, and others were employed in the various artist projects under the WPA.

This combination of art and activism is best exemplified by the unionization of many Hollywood players. The Screen Actors Guild (SAG) was founded in 1933. The Directors Guild of America was founded (as the Screen Directors Guild) in 1936. Throughout the 1930s, screen animators attempted to organize and met with limited success. Their strikes, however, did feature some of the best picket signs ever seen at a strike with favorite cartoon characters saying union slogans.

The Popular Front and the other aspects of the Great Depression era culture make it one of the most vibrant times of American culture. It was not a monolith of leftist propaganda, nor was it simply a time of looking backward, idealizing an American way of life that never really existed. The harsh realities of the time had a great effect on the materials produced in many different genres and art forms. By investigating the culture of the period, we are given a different lens by which we can understand the complexities of the Great Depression and those that experienced it.

Chapter 7: Sports and the Great Depression

Sporting heroes of the 1930s reflected a departure from the glamor of the heroes of the 1920s. Babe Ruth ended his career in 1934, and the baseball player who became the face of baseball couldn't be more different than Ruth. Lou Gehrig was everything that Ruth wasn't. Quiet, reserved, Gehrig went about baseball much more like a workman than a diva. During the 1930s, the number of games that Gehrig played consecutively earned him the nickname, "The Iron Horse." It was that aspect of Gehrig that especially made him so popular during the Depression. His dedication to his job and not taking a day off inspired others to not only appreciate his hard work but to find inspiration from his steady example. When having a job was a victory in and of itself, being steadfast like Gehrig was seen as the ideal.

But Gehrig was more than a simple workman. He was one of the elite players of his era. At first with Babe Ruth, then without the famed slugger, Gehrig led the Yankees to three consecutive World Series championships. He was the league's most valuable player in 1936. He was still playing at a high level in 1937, but there was a considerable drop-off in 1938, and then the unthinkable happened in 1939. Lou Gehrig told his manager to remove him from the starting lineup for the benefit of the team. The Iron Horse couldn't answer the call.

The diagnosis of amyotrophic lateral sclerosis (ALS) shocked the nation. Not only was it a very rare disease, but its debilitating effects were the antithesis of the way Gehrig had approached his craft. A man known for his durability and strength was literally wasting away. Gehrig, however, became perhaps even more of a hero as he faced his future. On July 4th, 1939, Gehrig gave one of the most memorable speeches in American history. The most famous image of the event was of Gehrig, looking frail and standing before the sellout crowd, telling them that he believed he was "the luckiest man on the face of the earth." Gehrig's grace in facing such adversity cemented his legacy as one of the most beloved sports figures of the 1930s and the twentieth century.

Baseball was still the most popular sport in the United States during the 1930s, and Gehrig was one of its biggest stars, representing the everyman with his work ethic. The St. Louis Cardinals and their famed "Gashouse Gang," on the other hand, represented an almost escapist perspective. Unlike the stalwart and businesslike New York Yankees and their leader Gehrig, the Cardinals were a fast and loose outfit, led by a group of brothers that almost sounded like the cast of a Marx Brothers film. Dizzy and Daffy Dean led the team, and as their nicknames suggested, they were more eccentric than the average baseball player. The 1934 team took on the brothers' eccentric persona, and other members of the team were given nicknames by the press as well. The team had a grubby appearance and played the game hard. They outlasted the New York Giants to win the National League and went on to win the World Series over the Detroit Tigers, 4 games to 3.

It was definitely the era of the hard worker. In addition to baseball figures, a horse also captured the imagination of the American people during the 1930s. Seabiscuit was an undersized, slightly below average horse for much of the early part of his career, but in 1936 he became almost unbeatable. Seabiscuit had some success on the eastern part of the racing circuit, but with a move out west, he starting winning handily. In 1937, he won 11 of the 15 races in which he was entered. Seabiscuit was the top money winner for the year as well. The winner of the Triple Crown that year, War Admiral, was named horse of the year.

In 1938, Seabiscuit had another successful year, even though his regular jockey had a series of serious injuries. At the end of the year, in what was called the "Race of the Century," Seabiscuit met War Admiral head-to-head at the Pimlico Race Track. It was a close race, with the lead changing from Seabiscuit to War Admiral on the backstretch. However, on the final 200-yard home stretch, Seabiscuit sped up and took the lead, eventually winning by four lengths. The race was well attended, with spectators jamming the infield, and it was broadcast on radio. It was the crowning achievement of Seabiscuit's career. The horse was retired in 1940 and put to stud for the rest of his life.

Seabiscuit was not the most graceful or beautiful horse, but in him, people saw a racer who worked harder than his competition and were inspired by his feats on the race track. Before his success in 1936, many of the established horse owners and trainers had given up on Seabiscuit, but his owner, Charles Howard, believed in him. Like so many heroes of the era, Seabiscuit was seen as an underdog, a racer who just needed a little faith and an opportunity to become a success.

 Similarly, James J. Braddock, the Cinderella Man, was not much of a fighter in the early part of his career but became a hero to many during the decade. Like so many Americans, Braddock struggled during the Depression to find steady work. It appeared his boxing career had ended with a broken right hand. Due to a late cancellation, Braddock was asked to fill in for another boxer. Defying the odds, Braddock won the bout, and over the next year put together a string of victories to earn a shot at the heavyweight title. Coming in as a 10-1 underdog, Braddock upset the champ, Max Baer, and won.

Braddock's appeal came from his rags to riches storyline, but also from the hard work he put in to achieve the title. When out of boxing, Braddock worked intermittently on the docks in New York and had difficulties at times providing food for his family. Braddock was also very frank when discussing his hardships prior to boxing and how lucky he was, inspiring countless fans with his story. Like Gehrig, Braddock was the everyman, the hard worker, and, like Seabiscuit, if given the chance, could do great things. More than anything, this was an ideal that workers in the Depression gravitated toward. Like their larger-than-life heroes, if given the opportunity, they could, on an albeit smaller scale, prove that they were worthy of employment and recognition.

Braddock held the heavyweight title for two years but didn't face any challengers in that time. When a contender did present himself, Braddock lost the title in his first defense. He was knocked out in the eighth round. It was the only time Braddock was knocked out outright, not a technical knockout. The hard-to-put-down Braddock met his match in one of the greatest boxers of all time, Joe Louis. Young and fast with devastating power, Braddock never stood a chance. "The Brown Bomber," as Louis came to be known, was a sensation.

Louis was part of the African American experience of the twentieth century. He was born in rural Alabama. When he was twelve years old, his mother, seeking better opportunities for her and her family, joined the thousands of African Americans moving to the industrial cities of the North as part of the Great Migration. His brother worked for Ford Motor Company and Joe did as well for a short time. Boxing, however, was his true calling. He began his amateur career at 17 and in two years debuted as a professional. Though not officially segregated, professional boxing was not exactly open to African Americans, who were often serious contenders for championships. Many within the white boxing community, promoters, managers, and fans alike, still resented the title reign of Jack Johnson, an African American fighter who challenged Jim

Crow laws and social mores by openly defying segregation policies and dating white women. In response, Louis and his management team strictly controlled his public image with the overall goal of gaining access to much more lucrative fights.

The strategy worked. By 1935, Louis was making his way up the rankings in the heavyweight division. He was also becoming the most popular athlete among African Americans. With each victory, African American communities across the country would celebrate "their champion." Louis' appeal, however, crossed racial boundaries. This was especially the case when fighting boxers from other countries, especially those that held decidedly un-American beliefs. The first fight that took on a political dimension was against former champion Italian Primo Carnera. To the public, Carnera represented the fascist government of Mussolini, who was in the process of invading Ethiopia. Louis was seen as the defender of democracy and of the small African country that was being invaded. Louis knocked Carnera out in six rounds, and it was seen as a symbolic victory for oppressed countries and for people of African descent. The greatest rival of Louis' career was also from a fascist country. The bouts between Louis and Max Schmeling became legendary.

Schmeling and Louis fought twice, in 1936 and 1938. Both fights had electric atmospheres with geopolitical implications. In the first fight, both fighters were top contenders for the heavyweight title, but neither held the championship at the time. Louis entered the fight on a 24-bout victory streak and took Schmeling lightly, not training nearly as vigorously as he normally did. Schmeling was ready and defeated Louis by knockout in the 12th of 15 rounds. Schmeling returned to Germany as a national hero and "proof" of the superiority of the Aryan race.

After Louis won the title from Braddock, the fight he needed to prove his legitimacy was a rematch with Schmeling. While the 1936 bout was a large event in its own right, the 1938 rematch is now remembered as one of the most historic sporting events of the twentieth century. Louis trained as hard as he ever had for the fight, wanting to put to rest any doubt that he was the best fighter in the world. In addition, Louis felt an immense amount of pressure to beat the representative of Nazi Germany. Even Franklin Roosevelt pressured Louis, saying that fighters like him were what was needed to beat Germany. For his part, Schmeling was accompanied by a Nazi official who proclaimed that it would be impossible for a black man to defeat the racially superior Schmeling.

Under such popular and political pressure, Louis delivered on all fronts. He defeated Schmeling in the first round, knocking him down three times. Schmeling's trainer saw enough of the beating and threw in the towel, ending the fight. Celebrations erupted across the nation, especially in African American communities. For many, it was vindication of racial equality that they had been striving for their entire lives. In a more general sense, it made Americans believe that despite their differences and hardships of the Depression the nation was strong and if need be able to fight in a war. Interestingly, when the United States entered World War Two, Louis enlisted as a private. Over the course of the war, he traveled over 20,000 miles, participating in countless boxing exhibitions and boosting morale for the United States forces.

Like Joe Louis, another African American athlete symbolically took on Nazism. The 1936 Olympics were held in Berlin, and the competition was intended to be a showcase for Adolf Hitler and his Nazi regime. Not only was the Olympics a chance to show the world how far Germany had come since the First World War, it was also a chance to demonstrate the genetic superiority of the Aryan race. Instead, Jesse Owens dominated the games like few athletes ever did. He won four gold medals, three in individual events and one in the 4 x 100 relay. Like the Louis victory over Schmeling two years later, African Americans saw Owens as an example of their racial equality and of the absurdity of racial segregation. It also exposed to many people around the world to the flawed logic of a superior race.

Some controversy still surrounds what happened after Owens won his medals in Berlin. It was reported at the time that Adolf Hitler snubbed Owens and his fellow African American winners. Owens later maintained that Hitler did not snub the competitors but instead needed to be elsewhere. Robert Vann, the editor for the African American newspaper *The Pittsburgh Courier* wrote that he saw Hitler wave to Owens as he left the stadium. Finally, one of Hitler's ministers wrote that Hitler was annoyed by the victories of non-Aryan people and believed such racers, who had an unfair physical advantage, should be banned from future games. All of these may be true to some degree. Owens didn't believe that Hitler snubbed him, and Hitler left the stadium to avoid further embarrassment of watching the "master race" continue losing.

What brought the hypocrisy of racial injustice to light was when Jesse Owens returned home from the Olympics. As the majority of African Americans were supporting Franklin Roosevelt in his bid for reelection in the fall of 1936, Owens refused, noting that the president didn't send any congratulations to him after his victories, nor did the president extend an invitation to the White House. Instead, Owens campaigned for FDR's Republican opponent, Alf Landon. Furthermore, while in Germany, Owens could move about freely, not segregated from the other Olympians. When he and his wife arrived at the Waldorf-Astoria Hotel in New York, Owens was refused at the front door, even though he was being honored for his Olympic victories. He was forced to enter through the kitchen entrance.

Perhaps the greatest athlete of the 1930s was an Olympic champion, Amateur Athletic Union (AAU) basketball All-American, and one of the greatest golfers of all time. Mildred Ella Didrikson, better known as Babe, seemed to be able to compete in any sport that she entered. She won two gold medals and one silver in track and field during the 1932 Summer Olympics. Capitalizing on her fame as an Olympic champion, Didrikson pitched in a number of major league spring training games in 1934. She also played with the barnstorming team from Michigan, the House of David. It was in 1935, however, that Didrikson found the sport that she was possibly best at, golf. Well before the founding of the Ladies Professional Golf Association (LPGA) in 1950, Didrikson was competing at an elite level on the links. In 1938, she entered the Los Angeles Open and is recognized as the first woman to compete in an event against men. Later in her career, she would enter three more men's tournaments and make the cut in two of them.

Didrikson was a pioneer for women athletics and she inspired future women. It wasn't just her prowess on the course or track oval that was inspiring. Even though she was a popular attraction while out touring, she also faced a great deal of discrimination. She was called unnatural and manly. Reporters often commented on her masculine looks and called her homely. Didrikson not only took it in stride but seemed to thrive on the comments. Like the other famous Babe from sports, Didrikson was bold and brash with a wit that bordered on ribald at times. She changed the way the public viewed female athletes, especially women golfers. She was not some petite society gal. Didrikson was strong, and she was proud to show her strength off to the crowds. It is commonly accepted that she had a lesbian relationship with one of her fellow golfers. Because of the social climate at the time, Didrikson was not able to be open about her sexuality. She was recognized as an LGBTQ pioneer by being inducted on the Legacy Walk in Chicago, Illinois in 2014.

Like other aspects of culture in the Depression, sports played a significant role in the lives of Americans. As a means of escape or inspiration, sports in the 1930s, like other forms of entertainment, provided a valuable means of coping with the realities of the economic crisis. The inspiration went beyond the personal and was inspiration for the nation as it became more and more involved in the currents leading to World War Two. Like other eras, the sporting heroes of the 1930s were a reflection of their time. Hard working and often underdogs, either in their sport (Braddock and Seabiscuit) or in society at large (Louis and Owens), the heroes of the 1930s were relatable to average Americans. People saw hard work paying off and wanted to believe that if they were given a chance, they could prove their worth like their idols.

Chapter 8: The Outlaw Celebrity in the Great Depression

American society and culture have a long history of interest in outlaws and criminals. From the days of the Western frontier until the Prohibition era, there was always an interest in the seedier side of American society. This interest continued and some argue reached a peak during the Great Depression. Especially in the Midwest and Mississippi Valley regions of the country, a fascination with outlaws catapulted some criminals from local celebrities to American legends that still capture our imaginations. Though the real motives of these criminals were far from altruistic, the popular appeal of them stemmed from the perception that they were rebelling against the power structure that many Americans saw as the real criminal. It is no surprise that the favored crime by so many of these lawbreakers was robbing banks. Sometimes operating as a gang and sometimes alone, all of these outlaws still resonate in popular culture.

In one case, it was more than just a criminal gang, but a family affair. After meeting in prison, Fred Barker and Alvin Karpis formed the Barker-Karpis Gang. Shortly after getting a crew together, Fred Barker brought in his brother, Arthur "Doc" Barker. Though there was a rotating cast of associates, the Barkers and Karpis decided which banks to rob. As their reputation grew, they decided that robbing banks had become too risky and decided to try their hand at kidnapping instead. In two high-profile cases, both involving men from the brewing industry, the Barker-Karpis Gang made off with close to $300,000 dollars.

The second kidnapping turned out to be the gang's undoing. The money used to pay the ransom had been sequenced by the FBI, and authorities were able to track down the criminals. It is here that another fascinating aspect of the gang came to light. When federal agents moved on the house where they were hiding, only Fred Barker and his mother were present. An hours-long shootout ensued. In the end, both Fred and Ma Barker were killed. Afterward, the FBI claimed that not only had the mother of the outlaw brothers participated in the fatal shootout but that she was the mastermind behind much of their criminal activity. There is no evidence that Ma Barker had anything to do with the crime spree of the gang, but the idea of it was too much for the public to abandon. Ever since her death in 1934, characterizations of Ma Barker have been a part of films and television. The dominant maternal figure within a crime organization has almost become an archetype.

The picture of a family engaging in a reign of terror was like a sinister version of the Joad family from *The Grapes of Wrath*. Instead of moving west looking for a better life, the Barker family stayed home and seized their own better life by taking it from the banks that had, in the eyes of many, caused the Depression. Even the kidnappings could be viewed as karmic payback. The first victim was William Hamm, son of the owner of Hamm's Brewing. The second victim was Edward Bremer, president of the Commercial State Bank and part of the Schmitt Brewing Company. Especially in the Midwest, brewing companies were some of the largest industries in the region. In Bremer's case, he not only represented big business, but the banking industry as well. While most people would never dream of committing such dastardly crimes, it was a bit of a voyeuristic fantasy to see the well-to-do be taken down a peg.

Another gang that caught the public attention due to the scandalous nature of their relationship was the criminal organization of Bonnie Parker and Clyde Barrow, better known simply as Bonnie and Clyde. Parker met Barrow in 1930 and soon joined up with his gang of outlaws. Over the next four years the Barrow Gang committed robberies and murders from Texas to Minnesota. Their exploits led to a large manhunt throughout the region and multiple gunfights with law enforcement.

It wasn't so much the criminal aspect of their relationship that intrigued the public so much as it was their romantic relationship. The idea of an outlaw couple on the run, engaging in explicit sex while not being married, was something right out of the pulp novels that were popular at the time. In addition, the gruesome details of their death only added to their mystique as criminal star-crossed lovers. Bonnie and Clyde were ambushed by law enforcement on a rural road in Louisiana, and the posse that attacked them fired over 120 rounds into their car.

In death, Bonnie and Clyde may have become even more famous. Over 20,000 people attended Bonnie Parker's funeral. Almost immediately after their deaths, the car they were killed in became a tourist attraction. It is still on display at a restaurant and casino outside of Las Vegas, Nevada. Every year on the anniversary of their deaths, thousands gather at the site of the ambush to celebrate Bonnie and Clyde.

The only criminal that rivals Bonnie and Clyde for enduring popularity is John Dillinger. Like Bonnie and Clyde and the Barkers, Dillinger was a bank robber by trade. It wasn't his robberies, however, that made him famous, but his exploits after he was captured. In the winter of 1934, Dillinger was transported from Arizona to Indiana to face trial for the crimes he committed in that state. On March 3rd, he escaped prison in Crown Point, Indiana. It is still debated how exactly Dillinger managed to do it. According to one account, he had smuggled a gun into his cell. According to the FBI, he carved a fake gun from a potato. Still others believe that he used a razor to carve a gun from the personal effects shelf in his cell. Regardless of the circumstances, Dillinger escaped and led the FBI on a manhunt throughout the upper Midwest.

It was during this time that Dillinger became a national sensation. Like the public feeling toward the robbing of banks as a kind of strike back at the powers that be, Dillinger staying one step ahead of law enforcement made him a kind of hero. The everyman, even if an outlaw, was outsmarting authority. What's more, rumors circulated that he was enjoying his time on the run. Living in Chicago, dating various women, and attending his favorite baseball team's games, The Chicago Cubs, made Dillinger into an almost Robin Hood type figure.

Like Bonnie and Clyde, Dillinger met a violent end and there was a touch of romantic scandal attached. When attending a movie with his girlfriend and a madam who was their mutual friend, the FBI was tipped off by said madam about where Dillinger was going to be. In order to ensure his identity, the madam wore a red dress (some accounts say orange) to point out the group. The infamous "Lady in Red" legend was born. Dillinger, not aware of the betrayal until it was too late, attempted to run down an alley by the theatre and was shot in the back.

Like Bonnie and Clyde, there was a fascination in John Dillinger after his death. People used newspapers and handkerchiefs to soak up his blood from the shooting site. Over 15,000 people came to view the body at the Cook County Morgue, and people still visit his grave in Indianapolis, Indiana.

In addition to the criminals becoming household names, the men who chased and arrested them also gained greater notoriety than law enforcement had previously. There were antecedents to the Federal Bureau of Investigation (FBI), but the agency was officially founded in 1935. The director of the FBI, J. Edgar Hoover, was at the forefront of law and order during the Depression and beyond. Starting during the Prohibition era and carrying on well past repeal of the eighteenth amendment, the FBI publicized their most wanted criminals. Dillinger, Karpis, and a host of other criminals were declared "Public Enemy Number One." With each arrest of the top fugitive, the next person was declared with as much press and fanfare as could be brought to bear.

The agents of the FBI acquired an almost heroic status. Called G-Men (Government Men), those that did the actual field work were revered by the population. One such agent, Melvin Purvis, became almost as well-known as Hoover. Purvis was part of the manhunts that brought in Pretty Boy Floyd, John Dillinger, and Baby-Face Nelson. There is some evidence that Hoover grew jealous of his agent's good press and undermined his career. Purvis resigned from the FBI in 1935 but wasn't finished with civil service. During World War Two, he served as a spy and gathered evidence against the Nazis at the Nuremberg Trials.

In contrast to the appeal of the outlaw, the G-Man was another hero for the time period. Just as there were people who were attracted to the aspect of the crimes attacking the well-to-do, there was also a need within the culture of the Depression for some semblance of order in a chaotic world. So, as people followed the misdeeds of the rogues' gallery of the 1930s, they were also counting on the upright heroes of law enforcement to bring order. Many of the movies of the era reflected this attitude. While the central characters were often criminals, they were always brought to justice in the end.

Chapter 9: Population Shifts and the Culture of the Great Depression

The Great Depression had a significant impact on the culture of the United States. Some of that impact was a result of the movement of large portions of the population across the country. Both movements had profound and lasting effects on American culture, well into the present day. The first, the movement of Southwesterners, largely to California, was largely the result of the devastation of the Dust Bowl. Okie culture, as it became known, made significant changes to California, and the Pacific Coast as a whole. The other movement during the Depression was a continuation of a movement that began during World War One and continued throughout the Depression, the migration of African Americans to the urban centers of the Midwest, Northeast, and later West altered not only the demographics of those cities but the politics and cultures of those cities as well.

The draw of California has been almost a constant pull in American life. The appeal of quick riches was the initial factor in the growth of the state, but people continued to migrate to the Golden State even after the gold rush had worn off. Until the 1930s and the environmental disaster of the Dust Bowl, the migration to California was steady, but not excessive. It also tended to be more of a middle-class phenomenon. As the dust blew across the heartland, however, the economic class was decidedly low. It wasn't necessarily the pull of California, but more of a move of desperation.

Though desperate, the migrants were looking for a better life. The majority of those who set out for California were young and male. Interestingly, though popularly thought of as mostly being rural farm workers, only about 36 percent of those that migrated were farmers. Over 50 percent of those that moved were from urban areas. Like other migratory movements, many of those who traveled did so because they already had relatives or contacts in the area. They moved to two distinct areas within the state, the cities, mostly Los Angeles, and the valleys, where farming was the main industry. Though collectively called Okies, the migrants largely came from four states, Oklahoma (naturally), Arkansas, Missouri, and Texas. California was the main destination for the people because the popular media and the state itself had been advertising the great opportunity that the state provided to the newcomer.

In reality, the idea of greater economic opportunity in California was well outdated by the time many from the Southwest moved. There was no more opportunity in the Golden State than there was anywhere else in the United States thanks to the Depression. Prior to the Depression, the state and local governments, especially that of the city of Los Angeles, were very welcoming of outsiders. After the economic downturn, however, native Californians became much less hospitable and even downright hostile to the Okies, a term used as a pejorative as the migration expanded. The Southwesterners were stereotyped by the native Californians as being strictly rural, backward folk, who were anti-modernism and lesser skilled than natives and other migrants. The Dust Bowl migration gave rise to the belief that there was a "tramp menace" in California, and in the mid-

1930s a group was founded, the California Citizens Association, to solve the migrant and transient problem that many perceived.

In the face of such discrimination, the Okies isolated themselves from the greater California population. In both the cities and rural regions, "Little Oklahomas" sprang up. While never the permanent neighborhoods such as a Little Italy or Chinatown, the Little Oklahomas were areas that Southwesterners clustered in. In such isolation, like other ethnic communities, members of the Okie subgroup found ways to conform to the dominant Californian culture. Children and the next generation were able to mix more freely, again much like ethnic children.

Like other enclaves, the Okies brought with them certain attitudes, customs, and cultures to California. The Southwesterners were very influenced by the populism of the early part of the twentieth century, and their anti-elitism and limited equality ethos were keys to their political outlook. It was a limited equality because, like those who remained in the Southwest, the tradition of racism was brought West. While a strong blue-collar sensibility and solidarity was present among the migrants, it only extended as far as their fellow whites.

Also affecting the political behavior of the newcomers was their evangelical religion. Many of the native Californian congregations were not welcoming to the Okies so they were forced to create their own faith communities. Especially influential were the Pentecostal or Holiness congregations. The preaching style and worship services were reminiscent of home for many of the migrants. It is a style of religious behavior that is still practiced across the country and gained a prominence it didn't have prior to finding roots in California.

In addition to the moral flavor of Okie culture, there was also a more secular side. Throughout California where Southwesterners settled, roadhouses and honky-tonks sprang up. For every evangelical spirit, there was also the "good old boy." The most prominent aspect of this is best represented in the music that became popular, namely country music. While the home of country music will always be Nashville,

Tennessee, the migrants from the Southwest brought their music with them. The influence of Okie culture could be seen, especially when sound became dominant in motion pictures. As mentioned in the previous chapter, Will Rogers was a native of Oklahoma. Gene Autry became famous as the singing cowboy. The culture of the Southwest was, and still is, a dominant aspect of popular culture.

Like the mass movement of Southwestern whites to California, the movement of African Americans from the rural South to the urban North was a significant demographic trend in twentieth-century US history. Termed the Great Migration, the movement of African Americans radically altered American cities and the South that they had left.

African Americans began moving during World War One when two key circumstances drove the migration. First, even though the US was not in the war, the industrial cities of the Northeast were desperate for workers because of the demands of the European belligerents. New York, Pittsburgh, Chicago, and many other cities had a labor shortage that needed to be met. Previously, companies often employed African Americans as strikebreakers, so there was some precedent for employing people from the South. In the case of the 1910s, it was just strikebreaking, but the need for more workers to meet demand. Often regulated to the worst jobs and the worst-paying jobs, it was still an opportunity that was often closed to African Americans.

The second key factor prompting African Americans to move to a strange new place was the continuing harsh conditions of the South. With the end of Reconstruction, whites in the South moved quickly to not only disenfranchise African Americans, but to limit them economically and socially. Between 1890 and 1910, all states in the former Confederacy held state constitutional conventions restricting access to the vote. Poll taxes, literacy tests, and comprehension tests, among other methods, were used to deny African Americans the right to vote.

In addition to voter suppression, economic and social restrictions were put in place to keep African Americans out of the power structure of Southern society. Laws were enacted to keep blacks and whites separate in all public areas. These laws were called Jim Crow laws, and they were found to be constitutionally acceptable by the Supreme Court in the 1896 ruling of *Plessy v. Ferguson*. In the court opinion, as long as accommodations were "separate but equal" then it was legal. The era of Jim Crow would last well into the 1960s.

Economically, African Americans found it almost impossible to own any property in the South, partly because they had no wealth post-slavery, but also because they had no means to accrue wealth after Reconstruction. The majority of former slaves either returned to their former plantations or found similar farming enterprises and entered into a very unfair economic practice of sharecropping. Through such a system, African American farmers were kept in a constant cycle of debt.

Those African Americans that were able to buy their own property were often intimidated or forced to give up their land or businesses, sometimes in a very brutal fashion. Over the course of the post-Reconstruction (1877) period through 1950, over 4,000 African Americans were lynched by white mobs. In every case, lynching was an extralegal method to intimidate the African American communities of the South. Mutilated bodies were left on display in order to terrorize African Americans and remind them of the power hierarchy at work in the South. Technically, African Americans were free from slavery, but Southern society looked remarkably like the society before the Civil War.

Added to the severe repression that African Americans dealt with in the postbellum South was an agricultural downturn that the region suffered in the 1910s. A series of poor cotton harvests then an infestation of the boll weevil devastated Southern agriculture. With little work available and many reasons to leave, the labor demand of World War One was a blessing for African Americans. During the war years, 1914-1918, close to half a million African Americans moved North. In the 1920s, over 800,000 African Americans made the move. The Great Depression slowed the migration, but still close to 400,000 people moved during the 1930s. By 1940, almost two million African Americans had moved from the South to the North.

Like the Okies in California, African Americans brought their culture with them to the cities of the North. African American food, religion, and music all had a strong impact on urban culture and the overall culture of the United States. Unlike the Okies, however, African Americans faced a great deal of discrimination and segregation in buying or renting properties in major US cities. In addition, many white institutions denied African Americans services in such areas as insurance, funeral homes, and medical services. These, among other small businesses, became the backbone of African American neighborhoods in cities like New York and Chicago. Serving the black community built a great deal of wealth for many African Americans, and they were able to translate this into financial and political power.

By the Great Depression, like so many other economic communities, the African American enclaves in cities were also hard hit. Upwards of 50 percent of black workers were unemployed in Chicago, Detroit, and Pittsburgh. However, in the South, African American unemployment reached as high as 70 percent. Many of the New Deal programs, including Social Security, offered little assistance to African Americans, but the neighborhood leaders of the North did their best to bridge the gap for the African American community. For example, Gus Greenlee, a prominent nightclub owner in Pittsburgh, provided turkeys and other groceries throughout the Hill District at Christmastime to families in need.

Though still harshly discriminated against throughout the United States, African Americans believed that Franklin Roosevelt was at least listening to their concerns. Roosevelt tripled the number of African Americans working in the federal government and appointed the first African American judge. A number of African Americans were tapped to act as special advisors to a number of cabinet members and they formed an informal "black cabinet," advising the president on issues affecting the African American community. One of the most famous members of this group was the close friend of Eleanor Roosevelt, Mary McLeod Bethune, a leading voice for African American women's rights. As the Depression was coming to an end because of the conversion to a war economy, Roosevelt issued one of the most significant executive orders of his presidency. Executive Order 8802 prohibited racial discrimination in the hiring practices of companies involved in the national defense industry. Though it was far from perfect and companies found ways to circumvent the order, it still provided a great deal of opportunity for African American workers.

By the end of the 1930s, the demographic picture of the United States had changed considerably. Over a million Americans had relocated in an attempt to find a better opportunity. African Americans continued a movement from the former Confederacy to the cities of the north. When the demand for labor again rose during World War Two, the largest movement of African Americans occurred when over 3 million people moved, including new destinations to the West, especially Los Angeles. During the Great Depression and after, Southern California was transformed by the amount of people moving in, but also by the culture these people brought with them. By the 1950s, California was as diverse as any state in the nation.

Chapter 10: International Issues and Concerns During the Depression

At the beginning of the Depression, the focus of the US government was, understandably, on domestic issues, especially the economy and the various crises facing the nation. Banking instability, unemployment, financial markets in ruins, and many other domestic issues were front and center during the Hoover administration and the first term of Roosevelt's presidency. The Great Depression was more than an American event, however. It was a global disaster that reached every part of the world. Like the United States, governments scrambled to find solutions to dire problems. In some cases, those solutions resembled the activities of the United States, by modifying capitalism, but not abandoning it. Nor did many countries abandon democratic and liberal government.

In Great Britain, the Depression wasn't as far of a fall as the United States experienced. Britain was still recovering from the First World War. When the stock market crashed in 1929, the famed economist John Maynard Keynes predicted that the crash would have little effect on London. As US trade diminished, the situation became more dire. The British government tried to keep trade afloat within the commonwealth countries and empire, by keeping tariffs low, but raising them abroad. Unfortunately, this had devastating effects. There was almost no demand for British products, and the industrial centers of Britain, especially the northeast of England, Wales and Northern Ireland, were particularly hard hit. In some areas, the unemployment rate reached 70 percent. At its worst, as many as 25 percent of the British population were living on a subsistence diet.

Unlike the United States, however, there were safeguards in place. There was a system of payment to the unemployed, called the dole. The British government also had national health insurance. Both of these programs started in 1911 and during the crisis of the 1930s were expanded to help more of the population. The increase in expenditures did slow any economic recovery, but Great Britain weathered the storm.

Meanwhile, the other western European ally from World War I, France, did not experience many of the problems that assailed Britain and America. Two key factors muted the effect of the Depression on France. First, France and French citizens did not have nearly the amount of capital invested in the world stock exchanges like English and Americans. Second, France did not have the massive industrial companies that dominated the economies of Britain and the United States. The French economy was decidedly smaller in scale, but when the crisis began, it was less open to vulnerabilities. French unemployment never reached the levels of the United States or Britain, and though there were economic hardships later in the decade, ultimately France survived the worst of the Depression with few scars.

The other ally of the war, Russia, was now the greater part of the Soviet Union. For the most part, its communist government was viewed with either outright hostility or at the very least suspicion. After Russia exited World War I, a civil war erupted within the country between the Red Army, led by Vladimir Lenin and Leon Trotsky, and the White Army, led by Russian military officers fresh from fighting Germany. Alexander Kolchak was a former admiral for czarist forces and Nikolai Yudenich a former general. The White Army was backed by the British and Americans. By 1923, the Red forces were victorious, but at great costs to Russia. The combined devastation of World War I and the Russian Civil War all but crippled the region.

After the civil war, leaders of the Red faction worked toward a consolidation of power, especially over numerous, smaller republics in Eastern Europe. As a result, much of Eastern Europe was under the control of Moscow and the communist leadership. Lenin was still the head of the communist regime, but his health was rapidly declining due to a series of strokes. Many had assumed Trotsky would be the new leader, but a younger member of the Communist Central Committee, Joseph Stalin, had been increasing his power within the party. After Lenin's death in 1924, despite a final statement by the former leader to elevate Trotsky and isolate Stalin from the committee, Stalin became the secretary general of the Soviet Union.

Stalin wasted little time in dispatching his enemies and former allies. By 1928, Trotsky was sentenced to eternal exile from the Soviet Union. During much of the 1920s, Stalin focused on restructuring the economy by having the state take complete control of industry and form collectives for agriculture throughout the Soviet Union. The policies weren't particularly popular, especially among the peasant farming class, but there was no denying the rise of Stalinism.

The drive to improve the economy and work toward full employment meant that when the Depression ravaged the Western democracies of the world, the Soviet Union was largely unscathed. In some instances, workers from Germany and the United States traveled to the USSR in search of work. During the 1920s and into the 1930s, workers were educated and given access to health care. Women were accorded the same rights, at least under the letter of the law, as men and were in the workforce at a much greater percentage. Perhaps most significantly, due to a program of immunizations for all children in the USSR, life expectancy rose by almost twenty years by the 1950s.

However, this progress hid a brutality that was truly staggering. Beginning in the 1930s, all organized religion was suppressed. During the Leninist era, the Orthodox Church was subject to persecution, but under Stalin all religions were suppressed. More staggering was the treatment of political enemies under Stalin. A number of trials, only for show purposes were conducted from 1936 through 1938 that purged all members of the party that had been a part of the Bolshevik Revolution in 1917. 1,108 of the 1,966 party officials with ties to the history of the USSR were arrested, put on a show trial, and either executed or exiled. Because of the ties of the Red Army to Trotsky, thousands of army officers were killed. Even Trotsky, living in exile in Mexico, was found in 1940 and assassinated. The purge extended to anyone who might be considered an enemy of the state—more precisely, an enemy of Stalin. Mass arrests, deportations, and internments were the norm in the Stalinist USSR. In one year alone, 1937-1938, close to 700,000 people were shot by the Soviet Secret Police, the NKVD.

Most of the death toll was kept from the rest of the world, but the trials of senior officials were widely reported. Many governments denounced the treatment of political prisoners and held that the court proceedings were a joke. The Communist Party of the United States (CPUSA), however, was split regarding the trials, with many members supporting Stalin and saying what was happening in the USSR was a necessary evil. Furthermore, the criticism of Stalin by Western democratic leaders was simply a matter of envy. Stalin and his nation were surviving, while the other nations of the world teetered on the brink. The strong support that much of the CPUSA showed Stalin severely hurt the organization, both in their membership and public perception.

Communism was one of three forms of political theory that dominated much of the post-World War One world. The United States, France, and Great Britain, among many other nations, represented liberal democracy and capitalism. Another philosophy, with roots in the nineteenth century, took shape in Italy after the war. Fascism was an authoritarian form of government that was on the far right of the political spectrum. In Italy, in the aftermath of the war, communist insurgents tried to organize left-leaning people, especially workers in the various industries throughout the peninsula. Benito Mussolini and the National Fascist Party he led used the unrest to subdue the strikers and gain favor with the industrialists of the country.

Gaining in popularity, especially among the armed services including local police forces, Mussolini continued to violently oppose workers' unions and socialists of any stripe. Eventually, the fascists didn't just attack party offices and member homes but took over entire cities. By the time Mussolini and his party moved on Rome in 1922, it was all but a fait accompli that he would become the undisputed leader of the country. At the end of October, the figurehead monarch of Italy officially appointed Mussolini prime minister. With the monarchy, industrialists, and even the Catholic Church supporting him, within three years Mussolini did away with the title of prime minister and declared himself Il Duce, or supreme leader.

Underlying fascism were a number of key ideas that, at least initially, were appealing to many, not only across Italy, but throughout the world. The enormity of the devastation from World War One repelled many, but some saw it as the new order of the world. The technological applications that were used to make war inspired some that a state of total war was achievable. In a fascist state, the goal was to be permanently mobilized. Fascism also relied heavily on mass enthusiasm. Large demonstrations, members wearing uniforms, and group activities (usually with violent outcomes) were measured ways to gain followers. In order to sustain such enthusiasm, a strong charismatic leader was needed.

From a more ideological perspective, fascism wasn't a reaction to the outcomes of World War One, where four major monarchies of the world were toppled, but to events prior to the conflict of 1914-1918. At its heart, fascism was a response to the Enlightenment and the French Revolution. Instead of believing in individual rights and the strength of reason, fascist doctrine embraced hierarchy, irrationalism, and emotionalism. The hierarchy extended beyond social order, such as supporting monarchies and other authority figures, but to a racial hierarchy as well. Mussolini was especially adroit at exploiting the fears of Italians about African migration.

Most importantly to fascism was the idea of the state. In a perfect nation, which would constantly be proving itself in war, the state and devotion to it was the pinnacle of being a good citizen. According to Mussolini in his work, *The Doctrine of Fascism* (1932), "The Fascist conception of the State is all-embracing; outside of it no human or spiritual values can exist, much less have value." The goal was to dominate the rest of the inferior world through warfare while the home country continued to produce the machines needed to make total war.

As the Depression overtook other Western European countries, Italy remained strong. Like France, Italy wasn't as dominated by massive corporations nor was the economy very dependent on the financial markets. The worldwide slowdown in trade hurt Italy as much as any country, but unemployment never reached the levels of the United States or Great Britain.

Like the Soviet Union and communism, Italy and fascism had its share of admirers. Many citizens were looking for an alternative to democracy and capitalism, and fascism seemed like a viable choice. Racial and ethnic tensions, along with a call for greater strength, resonated with people all over the world.

Nowhere was the appeal of fascism greater than in Germany. After World War One, the German nation was in an utterly dismal state. The people were near starvation; the economy was in shambles, their structure of government destroyed, and to top it all off, they were defeated by a long-standing enemy. The sense of humiliation and shame was palpable in Germany after the war.

With the Kaiser's abdication of the throne, the structure of the German government needed to be totally overhauled. As part of the Treaty of Versailles, the German delegation agreed to establish a democratic republic in the newly redrawn German state. For the first time, many regions of Germany had an electoral process. The Weimar Republic was tasked with guiding Germany through the painful process of recovery from the war.

Immediately after the war, recovery probably seemed impossible. Conditions were terrible, and an entire generation of men had been taken by the ravages of war. But by the middle of the 1920s, Germany was showing decidedly positive growth. German industry was among the largest in Europe, and cultural life was flowering under the Weimar Republic. Berlin was the place to be in Europe, and though the nation was still recovering, foreign investment was returning.

The Weimar Republic wasn't perfect and it had its fair share of critics from both sides of the political aisle. Communists and socialists tried to work with and undermine the government, depending on the situation. On the opposite side of the political divide was a new party, the National Socialist Party, better known as the Nazi Party.

At first, the Nazis did not gain much traction among the German people. It was made up largely of disgruntled veterans of the war and radicals who believed the Weimar government was forced on them, regardless of the government's current success. Quite influenced by the events in Italy and the message of Mussolini, the Nazis tried to emulate the Italian success of marching on Rome. The Nazis tried to take over the government through an attack on Munich. The Beer Hall Putsch of 1923 was the first attempt by the Nazis to try and take over the government of Germany. It failed miserably. The leader of the party, Adolf Hitler, was imprisoned for 18 months for the attempted coup. While in prison, Hitler wrote *Mein Kampf* which, like Mussolini's *Doctrine*, outlined what Hitler believed. Unlike Mussolini's work, it wasn't a reflection, but a forecast. Hitler was released from prison and decided a full-on paramilitary attack was not the way to advance his agenda. Instead, he and the Nazi Party decided to work through the Weimar system and wait for an opportunity.

The Depression was particularly harsh in Germany. It was the hardest hit nation of Western Europe. Germany had spent the last decade building its industrial strength, and when world trade slowed to a standstill, the German economy ground to a halt as well. The global crisis produced fertile ground for the Nazi Party to campaign and share their ideas. At their heart, the Nazi principles reflected the same notions as Italian fascism. A strong leader was needed to end the current state of affairs. Furthermore, Germany was destined for greatness, if only it hadn't been betrayed by the premature end of the war. Hitler and the Nazis perpetuated the idea that their main political opponents, all liberal democrats within Weimar, were "November criminals" who sold Germany out to France and Great Britain.

The idea of social and racial hierarchy was also a key element of the Nazi message. The fear and prejudice that the Nazis tapped into was against Jews living in Germany. In addition to the ethnic minority of the Jews, the Nazi Party also targeted other political parties that were attempting to disrupt Germany as well. Like the Italian fascists, the Nazis were seen as the better alternative to the socialists and communists. By 1930, the message was working. The Nazi Party gained enough votes to become the second largest political party in Germany.

The Depression worsened in Germany as the number of unemployed workers rose from 4 million to 5.6 million in 1931. The disillusionment that the people had for the Weimar government increased, and by 1932, the Nazi Party was the largest political party in Germany, dominating the German legislature, the Reichstag.

Centrist and conservative politicians believed that if they included Hitler in their coalition government, they could perhaps control him, and by extension, the rest of the Nazi Party.

The Nazis, however, proved to be too powerful to control, including Hitler. After being named chancellor in 1933, Hitler and his lieutenants moved swiftly to consolidate their power through all levels of government. After a mysterious fire burned down the Reichstag, Hitler was given emergency, almost absolute, powers to deal with the crisis. Political opponents were arrested, and the Gestapo, the secret police of the Nazi era, was formed. By the end of the year, the Nazi Party was declared the only legal political party in the country.

Political hegemony was almost complete by the end of 1933 for Adolf Hitler. It is often pointed out that Franklin Roosevelt and Hitler came to power in the same year, though by very different means. In 1934, while Roosevelt was working to get the New Deal through Congress, Hitler was finishing his agenda of becoming the supreme leader, the Führer of Germany. Hitler won over the military of Germany by giving the army almost complete autonomy. He also promised to dissolve one of the paramilitary organizations within the Nazi Party, the SA, or brownshirts. What had started as little more than an honor guard in the early days of the Nazi party, the SA had become a powerful organization in its own right, rivaling the army in manpower. In the summer of 1934, the Night of Long Knives occurred. The leader of the SA and many of his most loyal officers were arrested and summarily executed. With the SA taken care of, the German army officer class agreed to back Hitler when the president of the country died and make him chancellor and president of Germany, the head of state and the head of government. This occurred sooner than many thought it would, and by the end of the summer of 1934, Hitler held both offices and took on the title of Führer.

As mentioned earlier, one of the main theories underlying fascism were the ideas of total war and military preparedness. To that end,

Hitler outlined an ambitious plan to rearm the German army. Even though such a course of action was prohibited by the Treaty of Versailles, Germany continued to build up their military while the rest of the world simply shrugged. Part of this might well have been because most Western countries saw Nazi Germany as a buffer between Russia and the rest of Western Europe. France and Great Britain were not in any condition either to oppose Germany's military build-up. The next phase of Nazi Germany was to reintegrate lands seized by the allies at the end of World War One back into Germany. The first such case was a small area between France and Germany, Saarland. The British and French agreed that if the residents of the area voted to rejoin Germany, then they would be allowed to do so. With a great assist from the Office of Propaganda in Germany, over 90 percent of the residents voted to rejoin Germany. The next attempts to regain territory were not as easy as a simple vote.

In order to fulfill the fascist vision of the world, the "greater" nations needed to eventually conquer the weaker ones. The first fascist country in Western Europe, Italy, was also the first to invade another country. In 1935, Italy, in an attempt to expand their world influence, invaded Ethiopia. The League of Nations was not able to stop the aggression of Italy, and the Western powers of France, Great Britain, not to mention the United States, did nothing. Taking this inaction as cowardice, Hitler moved German troops into the Rhineland territory of Germany. This was another blatant violation of the Treaty of Versailles. It was apparent that Hitler had little regard for the treaty.

The militarization of the Rhineland was cause for concern, but what gained even more attention, especially among the left in the United States, was the outbreak of the Spanish Civil War. General Francisco Franco led a military coup against the republican government of Spain and was intent on bringing a fascist regime to power on the Iberian Peninsula. Franco had powerful allies, including Germany who sent troops in the form of the Condor Legion, Italy, and

Portugal. Opposing the insurgents along with the Spanish republicans were troops from the Soviet Union, France, and the United States, though the US contingent was not officially recognized by the Roosevelt administration. For many in the CPUSA, the fighting in Spain was of vital importance. It was the first real chance to stop the spread of fascism. It also coincided with the principles of the Popular Front. Not everyone fighting for the republic was a communist, but it was a demonstration of a coalition fighting against the greater threat of fascism. The Americans who went to Spain were organized as an international brigade. They took the name the Lincoln Brigade because they were fighting for the survival of the Spanish Republic, similar to Lincoln's fight in the American Civil War. Of the 3,000 volunteers that went overseas, 681 were killed.

It is important to mention that all international tension in the world was not focused on Europe. Throughout the 1930s, tensions between the United States and the Empire of Japan were constantly high. Japanese militarism, much like that of Italy and Germany, went unchecked by the League of Nations. Japan first invaded the Chinese region of Manchuria in 1931. As civil war erupted in China between communist and nationalist forces, Japan exploited the division and gained territory throughout the province. The amount of skirmishing in the region was cause for worldwide concern, but little action came of it. Great Britain, the largest western power in the region, was reluctant to send troops to Asia because of the growing fear of a European conflict. France felt the same, and the United States military was not considered strong enough to be of any real threat. Weighing all of these factors, Japan committed fully to the action in China and a formal declaration of war was issued in July of 1937.

The worldwide tensions of the late thirties touched every nation, including the United States. The growing rivalry between two extreme forms of government, fascism and communism, put the United States squarely in the middle of the global stage. Various factions within the United States supported each side of the overarching conflict. Many on the left supported the Soviet Union, and other organizations demonstrating their support of Germany. Still, others in the United States, especially in the late thirties, wanted to stay completely out of any and all conflicts. Isolation was the watchword for most Americans. How long such a stance could remain tenable was the question that Roosevelt had to consider.

Chapter 11: The Coming Storm and the End of the Depression

On December 7, 1941, the United States was attacked at the naval base at Pearl Harbor in the United States territory of Hawaii. By the end of that week, the United States was at war on two fronts. One was largely based in the Pacific Ocean, fighting the Empire of Japan. The other was on the continent of Europe against the nations of Germany and Italy. The majority of the belligerent nations had been at war since 1939, 1937 in Asia. The United States had remained largely out of the fray, at least when it came to actual troops on the ground. As far as choosing sides and providing aid, the Americans had largely made their intentions known. Even before the US officially entered the war, the war was having an impact on the country. As the second term of Franklin Roosevelt's presidency continued, the greatest conflict of the twentieth century was stirring. It was only a matter of time before it reached across the two oceans and brought the Western Hemisphere into the conflict.

As Roosevelt's second term continued, the American economy was showing great signs of improvement. Unemployment had fallen to under 15 percent, and manufacturing was up, as was per capita earnings. By the fall of 1937 and through most of 1938, unemployment rose again, almost to 20 percent. Manufacturing output fell by over a third. There was great concern that the nation was beginning to slip back into the depth of the Depression.

Blame was quick to spread between business-oriented conservatives and liberal New Dealers. The business advocates expressed that it was because of the New Deal's inherent prejudice toward corporate interests that recovery would always be retarded. The advocates of the New Deal countered that it was because of FDR abandoning parts of the New Deal, especially when it came to spending. FDR was concerned with balancing the budget and did not want to rely on deficit spending any longer than was necessary. Also, blaming the New Deal and Roosevelt was easy because the president and his administration were quick to take credit for any signs of recovery. Receiving criticism when things went poorly was the second edge to that particular sword.

In reality, the Roosevelt Recession, as it became known, was probably due to the natural business cycle more than any other reason. At the time, however, the two sides blamed one another. Roosevelt himself thought that it was a concerted effort by key Republicans and business leaders trying to create another depression so people would turn against the Democrats in the coming election. He had the FBI investigate numerous business families for collusion. Nothing was ever found. The Roosevelt administration also took more tangible steps to stop the slide. A large spending bill was sent to Congress in 1938 that, like earlier programs, infused the economy with money. While unemployment and production didn't reach the poor levels of early 1937, the recession was all but stopped. Events abroad, especially in Europe, spurred production in the United States.

After Germany reoccupied the Rhineland in the spring of 1936, Hitler moved to improve his image and position on the world stage. First was the great pageant of the 1936 Olympics in Berlin. The German capital never looked better. Though it was more veneer than substance, the Olympics were a showcase for Germany and especially Hitler. Later that year, Germany and Italy signed an alliance, which according to Mussolini would result in the rest of Europe to "rotate on the axis between Berlin and Rome." Later that same year in November, Germany and Japan signed the Anti-Comintern Pact to stop the spread of the Soviet Union and communism around the world. Though it was still years in the future, the Axis Powers were now linked together.

Though both Germany and Japan saw themselves as the true power in their alliance, both were also willing to allow the other their own sphere of influence, Germany in Europe and Japan in Asia. The United States and the Western Hemisphere were not much of a concern. Italy, however, was decidedly a junior partner from the beginning. The goals for Europe were predominantly German goals. Italy and Mussolini were more or less along for the ride.

Even before the annexation of the Rhineland, a key component of the Nazi agenda was the concept of Lebensraum, or living space, for the German people. After World War One, a large portion of Germany was divided up among the victorious nations. As Hitler rose to power and influence in the world, his call for a larger Germany found many sympathetic ears, hence the lack of reaction to the seizure of the Rhineland. The next part of this agenda was to unite Germany with the other former great Germanic nation, Austria. Like Germany, Austria had suffered defeat in World War One. In a demonstration of strength and solidarity, the German army marched into Austria unopposed. It was reminiscent of a Roman triumph, except in the streets of Vienna. The Anschluss, which means joining, was completed in the spring of 1938. In two years, Germany had extended its sphere of influence from the Rhine to the Danube.

German expansion wasn't over. In the fall of 1938, Hitler made his intentions clear about territory boarding Czechoslovakia, referred to as the Sudetenland. In order to protect ethnic Germans living in the territory, Hitler was prepared to invade Czechoslovakia. The rest of Europe opposed such action, but were also opposed to another major war. Great Britain, France, Germany, and Italy met in order to stave off war. On September 30, 1938, the Munich Agreement was signed by the four aforementioned countries. The agreement stipulated that Germany would be allowed to take over the Sudetenland, provided that they would not invade the rest of Czechoslovakia. The Czech people and government were appalled and felt betrayed. A quick look at the map shows that the remaining Czech territory was all but surrounded by a hostile neighbor. The British Prime Minister Neville Chamberlain infamously said that the agreement would result in "peace in our time." In less than a year Great Britain would again be at war with Germany.

The United States was not eager to become engaged in another European war either. In the almost 20 years after the end of World War I, many Americans questioned whether or not the Unites States should have been involved at all. As Germany became more and more belligerent, the US Congress began passing "Neutrality Acts" to ensure that the country would not be pulled into another conflict. The ultimate goal of the acts was to keep United States corporations from selling war materials to hostile nations. Roosevelt was opposed to the acts because he believed it would hurt nations that were friendly toward the United States. As the Spanish Civil War intensified and Germany began its expansion, the 1937 renewal of the Neutrality Acts contained a provision meant to please the president and prevent him from possibly vetoing the act. The "cash and carry" stipulation in the 1937 Neutrality Act allowed countries to trade with the United States, with the exception of munitions, if they took the supplies in their own boats and paid cash up front. Since Britain and to a lesser extent France were the world powers at sea, it meant that the Western democracies and not Germany would most likely be the nations to be a part of the cash and carry program.

Roosevelt was going against the current for much of the late 1930s. Many Republicans and Southern Democrats were staunch isolationists, even as the world slipped further and further into war. In 1937, the same year cash and carry was adopted, Roosevelt gave his "quarantine" speech. He stated that the United States needed to quarantine aggressive nations around the world in order to protect US interests. If he had hoped to inspire a more international concern, Roosevelt failed. It seemed to only intensify the isolationist mood of the country. Even as Germany took the Sudetenland and in 1939 the rest of Czechoslovakia, the US Congress passed another Neutrality Act and refused to extend cash and carry.

As 1939 progressed, the threat of a full-scale war increased with each month. The next target of German expansion was Poland. Much to the disbelief of the world, especially communists living outside of the Soviet Union, the USSR and Germany signed a nonaggression treaty. The agreement pledged both powers not to invade the other for 10 years. Secretly, the Soviet Union and Germany agreed to split up Eastern Europe in the coming years. Hitler was assured that the Soviets would not resist the invasion of Poland. Even without knowledge of the secret agreement, the Communist Party of the United States was divided and lost a great deal of credibility and support among many others on the left in US politics.

In August 1939, the British signed a treaty with Poland promising to fight on their behalf in case of invasion. It did not take long for the agreement to take effect. On September 1, 1939, Germany invaded Poland, starting World War II. Along with the British, the French came to the aid of the Polish. There was little chance to provide aid. Warsaw, the capital of Poland, surrendered on September 27th.

While the British and French had declared war on Germany, they did very little to prevent the quick defeat of Poland. The two Western powers were waiting for Germany to turn its attention toward the west. They did not have to wait for long. The following spring, in 1940, the Germans advanced across the north of Europe, seizing Denmark and Norway in April and moving through Belgium, the Netherlands, and ultimately France by June of 1940.

As Europe fell under German rule, many Americans were still opposed to getting involved. As the British faced a fierce German air assault, remembered as the Blitz, the America First Committee was founded in the United States. The group opposed any intervention by the US government. The group grew to almost 1 million members by 1941. However, the American people were in favor of Britain winning its battle against Germany. There was a great deal of support for aiding Great Britain by all means short of becoming a participant in the war.

To that end, Roosevelt proposed a program for lending nations opposed to Germany and Japan war materials. Roosevelt likened it to lending a neighbor a hose to douse a fire. In theory, the nations that borrowed the materials would return it to the United States. In reality, very little was returned and no one really expected it. The program became known as the Lend-Lease program. Once the US officially entered the war, the United States military was granted no-cost leases among many of its allies as a means of exchange for all of the goods provided.

With the advent of Lend-Lease, the idea of American neutrality was all but dead. As Roosevelt proclaimed about the program, it meant that the United States was the "Arsenal of Democracy." Though the economy wasn't officially a war economy, it practically was. The unemployment rate fell below 15 percent for only the second time since the Depression had started in 1940. By 1941, it would fall below ten percent for the first time since 1930. The United States was out of the Depression, hopefully for good. Just like the Depression, however, the years immediately after the Depression were marked by just as much sacrifice and dedication as the previous decade.

The discussion of isolation and neutrality all but ceased on December 7th, 1941. The Japanese attack on Pearl Harbor was one of the most devastating attacks on a US-held territory. No contemporary of the time could recall a similar event. While there were outliers throughout World War II, the overwhelming majority of Americans were in favor of entering the war. The attack on Pearl Harbor was a surprise to most Americans, but US policies in Asia made such an attack from Japan, not the other Axis Powers, more likely.

As early as 1937, when Japan invaded China, relations between the United States and Japan were strained. The United States almost immediately declared that they supported China in the conflict. The Neutrality Acts of the 1930s limited who the US would and would not trade with; Japan was one of the first nations to be cut out of trade with the US. Important steel, oil, and other materials needed for the war effort of Japan were no longer available from the United States. By 1940, the United States was overt in their support of China against the Japanese, training soldiers and pilots and supplying them war materials through the Lend-Lease program.

For much of 1941, the United States and Japan held negotiations to ease tensions between the two countries and to also bring about a resolution to other conflicts in Asia. It appeared that de-escalation was possible. After Germany invaded Russia in the summer of 1941, the Japanese high command saw their chance to push south toward the Dutch East Indies and sent over 100,000 troops to Indochina. The United States reacted swiftly and harshly. The US froze all Japanese assets in US banks. Roosevelt also ordered all troops on the Philippines be brought under US control. As a final punishment, the US denied the Japanese use of the Panama Canal.

As might be expected, diplomatic relations between the two countries were almost non-existent for the rest of 1941. Military command in the United States was sure there would be an attack on some US holding in the Pacific. Most experts agreed that the attack would be on Midway, Wake Island, Guam, or perhaps even the Philippines. No one thought the Japanese would venture as far away as Hawaii and the home of the US Pacific fleet.

War was declared by the US Congress against the Empire of Japan on December 8th, 1941. Shortly thereafter, Germany and Italy declared war on the United States and the US responded in kind. The United States was already emerging from the Great Depression before the official declaration of war thanks to the industrial needs of the Lend-Lease Program. However, with the US officially in the conflict, unemployment fell below 5 percent for the first time since 1929 and would fall below 2 percent for the remainder of the war. As the need for soldiers rose throughout the war, segments of the population not usually tapped for industrial work were employed, most notably women. After twelve years of economic hardship, the Great Depression was finally over.

Conclusion

When victory was finally declared in September of 1945, the mood of so many Americans was understandably celebratory. The United States defeated two threatening foes and, to paraphrase the departed FDR, preserved the world for democracy. In addition, the United States was the only major combatant that didn't suffer great destruction of its infrastructure and population centers. In many ways, the United States was the last man standing after a terrible, costly war.

However, that position carried with it a set of fundamental concerns, most notably what was going to happen with the war ending. The greatest fear of many in the Truman administration was the return of the depression. Soldiers were returning by the thousands, eager to find employment and begin a new life after surviving the crucible of war. Those that had worked in the factories and fields, the active participants in the "Arsenal of Democracy," weren't ready to vacate those jobs, even if that was the expectation. The vision of hundreds of thousands of unemployed soldiers crowding into cities and across the countryside filled many with a sense of urgency.

The generation that lived through the Depression and fought in the war now needed to sustain the wartime economy in order to ensure that another economic collapse did not occur. Through the Truman and Eisenhower administrations, great federally funded programs bolstered the economy or prepared the returning soldiers to enter the workforce. Key programs from the New Deal, especially Social Security, were enhanced and expanded. By the 1960s, Medicaid and Medicare would follow in the footsteps of the original Social Security Act. Lyndon Johnson's domestic initiatives to end poverty, called the Great Society was the direct descendant of the New Deal. Those that lived through the Depression were determined to not let it happen again.

In much the same way, working-class Americans, those that felt the brunt of the Depression more severely than anyone else, were determined to ensure their economic stability as well. Instead of demanding a greater voice in management and the means of production, American unions focused on establishing and preserving their members economic and future well-being. Unions demanded strong health insurance and pensions from their employers. Workers were also able to make great gains in wages and, coupled with generous FHA loans or loans through credit unions, were able to buy housing of their own.

The economic lessons of the Great Depression haven't been totally forgotten. The economic recession of 2008 served as a painful reminder. Unlike 1929, the government, another Republican administration ironically, acted swiftly to stave off a total collapse. While the economy slowed down dramatically in 2008, it never approached the dire situation of the 1930s. The Great Depression still looms large in the American consciousness. As debates over tariffs and restructuring Social Security continue to rise, let's hope that the Great Depression still affects thinking and policy in the future.

Here are some other Captivating History books that you might be interested in

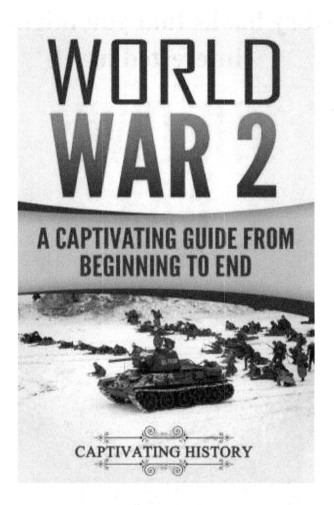

WORLD
WAR 2

A CAPTIVATING GUIDE FROM
BEGINNING TO END

CAPTIVATING HISTORY

THE ROARING TWENTIES

A CAPTIVATING GUIDE TO A PERIOD OF DRAMATIC SOCIAL AND POLITICAL CHANGE, A FALSE SENSE OF PROSPERITY AND ITS IMPACT ON THE GREAT DEPRESSION

CAPTIVATING HISTORY

AFRICAN AMERICAN HISTORY

A CAPTIVATING GUIDE TO THE PEOPLE AND EVENTS
THAT SHAPED THE HISTORY OF THE UNITED STATES

CAPTIVATING HISTORY

References

Brinkley,Alan. *The End of Reform: New Deal Liberalism in Recession and War.* New York, Vintage Books, 1995.

Cohen, Lizbeth. *Making A New Deal: Workers in Chicago 1919-1939.* Boston, Cambridge Press, 1990.

Denning, Michael. *The Cultural Front: The Laboring of American Culture in the Twentieth Century.* New York, Verso Publishing, 1996.

Douglas, Ann. *Terrible Honesty: Mongrel Manhattan in the 1920s.* New York, Farrar, Straus and Giroux, 1996.

Erenberg, Lewis. *Swingin' In the Dream: Big Band Jazz and the Rebirth of American Culture.* Chicago, University of Chicago Press, 1998.

Kennedy, David. *Freedom From Fear: The American People in Depression and War, 1929-1945.* London, Oxford Press, 2001.

May, Lary. *The Big Tomorrow: Hollywood and the Politics of the American Way.* Chicago, University of Chicago Press, 2000.

Peretti, Burton. *The Creation of Jazz: Music, Race, and Culture in Urban America.* Chicago, University of Illinois Press, 1994.

Pells, Richard. *Radical Visions and American Dreams: Culture and Social Thought in the Great Depression.* Chicago, University of Illinois Press, 1973.

Susman, Warren. *Culture as History: The Transformation of American Society in the Twentieth Century.* Washington DC, Smithsonian Books, 1984.

Free Bonus from Captivating History (Available for a Limited time)

Hi History Lovers!

Now you have a chance to join our exclusive history list so you can get your first history ebook for free as well as discounts and a potential to get more history books for free! Simply visit the link below to join.

Captivatinghistory.com/ebook

Also, make sure to follow us on:

Twitter: @Captivhistory

Facebook: Captivating History:@captivatinghistory

Made in the USA
Middletown, DE
12 February 2025

71286120R00056